AF526745

Nature as Reflected
in
the Art and Architecture
of
KHAJURAHO
(AND OTHER CHANDELLA SITES)

Nature as Reflected in the Art and Architecture of KHAJURAHO (AND OTHER CHANDELLA SITES)

S.K. Sullerey

ABI Prints & Publishing Co.
New Delhi

NATURE AS REFLECTED IN THE ART AND ARCHITECTURE OF KHAJURAHO
(AND OTHER CHANDELLA SITES)

ISBN: 978-81-86787-17-5

© S.K. Sullerey, 2011

All rights reserved. No part of this book may be reproduced or transmitted in any form or by any means, electronic and mechanical, including photocopy, recording or any other information storage and retrieval system or otherwise, without written permission from the publisher.

Published in **2011** by
ABI PRINTS & PUBLISHING CO.
Pooja Apartments, 4B, Ansari Road, Darya Ganj, New Delhi-110 002 (India)
Tel.: 23287589, 23255799; Fax: 91-11-23270385
E-mail: aryanbooks@gmail.com
www.aryanbooks.co.in

Printed in India at Mudrak, Delhi-110091

Preface

The Chandellas of Jejakabhukti (Present Bundelkhand region of U.P. and M.P.) were great rulers, warriors and builders of their times. They protected their kingdom twice from the attacks of Muhmud of Ghazni. They ruled over Jejakabhukti region for about six centuries, an unusual period in the annals of ruling dynasties of early medieval India. Their cultural achievements were more significant than their political achievements. They adorned their kingdom with forts, palaces, temples, tanks, lakes and parks, which were mainly centred in the cities of Mahoba (U.P.), Kalanjara (U.P.) and Ajaigarh (M.P.) and to a lesser degree in the towns of Dudhahi, Chandpur, Madanpur and Deogarh. But none of these places could be compared in magnificence with Khajuraho, which was decorated by the Chandellas with temples, tanks and lakes. According to literary tradition, the place had originally eighty-five temples, but only twenty-five now remain in different stages of preservation. Khajuraho is one of the finest creation of Chandellas. The existing temples of Khajuraho built during the reign of the Chandellas offer interesting study of art and architecture. In the sculptural art of Khajuraho every aspect of human life – from birth to decay – every phase of our imagination, realistic or otherwise, is depicted with great delicacy through the chisel of the artists of Chandella kingdom. The entire history of a section of Indian people, their habits and manners, their joys and sorrows, their religion and culture, could be seen on the temple walls with glaring vividness.

The temples of Khajuraho are not inchoate blocks of stone, kept one over the other but they are living monuments of great inspiration of singing the symphony of life for centuries to come.

The region of Madhya Pradesh, where Khajuraho is situated, is rich in natural surroundings, which inspired Chandella artists to create great monuments of world heritage. Much work has been published by many art historians and art critics on different aspects of Chandella art and architecture. But no attempt has been made so far to study the reflection of environment on the Chandella art and architecture. An attempt has been made in the present volume to study the reflection of environment on the basis of literary and archaeological sources.

The present monograph is the outcome of a study under a project entitled, *Environment as Reflected in Chandella Art and Architecture (with special reference to Khajuraho)* approved by the Indian Institute of Advanced Study, Shimla. It comprises of an introduction and seven chapters along with maps and photographs related to the project. The Introduction contains importance and justification of topics concerned and also sources pertaining to the research project. Similarly, it also comprises the review of work already done from 19th century AD to 21st century AD. While reviewing the work already done in the field of Chandella history and art history, I found that art historians overlooked the environmental reflections on Chandella art and architecture.

In the present project an attempt has been made to study the rock-cut art and architecture that flourished during the Chandella period at Ajaigarh, Kalanjara, Mahoba and Deogarh. The present study is confined to the main centres of Chandella art and architecture – Ajaigarh, Kalanjara and Mahoba, with special reference to Khajuraho. It dwells on those aspects which are closely associated with the environmental aspects related to art studies.

The monograph is divided into seven chapters. The first chapter contains the geo-political study of Jejakabhukti region over which Chandella art and architecture flourished. The geographical environment to a large extent influenced the life and culture of the region. The geographical factors are reflected in the Chandella art and architecture in various ways. The geographical location provided them building material such as rocks and stone slabs which were available in the region. The Chandella artists utilized rocks for construction of tanks, ponds, caves, temples and vivid sculptures at Ajaigarh, Kalanjara and Mahoba.

The Panna stone quarries of sandstone provided ample material to the Chandella artists for construction of magnificent temples at Khajuraho. Similarly, the diamond mines of Panna gave richness to Chandella rulers for the construction of extraordinary temples at Khajuraho and other places in their kingdom. Thus, the geographical environment provides a basis for study of Chandella art and architecture.

The Chandella rulers were great builders of their time. They patronised art and architectural activities in their kingdom and for the study of chronology of the temples, political history is indispensable.

The second chapter contains natural surroundings of the main centres of Chandella art and architecture. The natural surroundings are reflected in temple architecture of Khajuraho in various decorative motifs. Similarly, the social features of the people are reflected in Chandella sculptures depicted at Khajuraho temples.

The third chapter is related with environmental geography. Environmental geography played a key role in the construction of monuments and selection of sites for the construction of temples. It inspired the artist to create beautiful surroundings of the temples.

The fourth chapter contains forestry and wildlife along with reptiles reflected in Chandella art and architecture. We find several depictions of forests and hunting scenes in which Chandella artists revealed the forestry and wildlife in a beautiful and realistic manner.

The fifth chapter contains animals and birds which were depicted in Chandella art and architecture. An attempt has been made to study in depth this aspect which is less studied by art historians.

The sixth chapter contains the study of water resources. The water resources are divided into two parts – natural water resources and excavated and constructed water resources. The water resources played a vital role in enhancing the beauty of the monuments. Water also played a significant role in the ritual life of the temples.

The seventh chapter is related with the conclusions. The creativity of the artists during the Chandella period articulated and inspired by the surrounding environment is reflected beautifully in their sculptural art.

We can conclude that every aspect is related to human life and the environment is beautifully reflected in Chandella art and architecture. In the words of Banabhatta, they are truly '*Darshit Vishwarupa*'. Firstly, I bow to the gods and goddesses of Khajuraho and other sites for their divine blessing and inspiration to complete this project successfully.

I express my heartiest gratitude to the past and present authorities of Indian Institute of Advanced Study, Shimla, for providing me an opportunity to pursue my project in the beautiful surroundings of heritage building presently known as Rashtrapati Nivas, Shimla. The Institute provided me all the basic amenities and an academic atmosphere to pursue my research project.

I also express my gratitude to the authorities of the Archaeological Survey of India, Bhopal Circle, for providing me beautiful photographs related to my project work.

I also acknowledge the help of the officials of A.S.I. working at the sites of Khajuraho, Kalanjara and Ajaigarh for helping me in my project work.

I express my gratitude to the authorities of the American Institute of Indian Studies, Gurgaon, for providing me some photographs related to my project work.

I express my thanks to the Librarian and his colleagues at IIAS, Shimla, for providing me all facilities related to my academic pursuit relating to books and journals. The administrative and all other staff of the Institute also helped and cooperated with me in various ways. I also express my heartiest thanks to them.

I express my thanks to my fellow colleagues and research associates coming from all parts of the country for inspiring me and helping me in my project.

May God bless the members of my family who assisted me and inspired me to complete this project. I heartily thank SMS Computer, Boileauganj, Shimla, for typing my monograph neatly and correctly.

Shimla **S.K. Sullerey**

Contents

List of Abbreviations

A.S.I.A.R. : *Archaeological Survey of India, Annual Report.*
A.S.I.R. : *Archaeological Survey of India Reports* by Alexander Cunningham.
C.I.I. : *Corpus Inscriptionum Indicarum.*
C.M.I. : *Coins of Mediaeval India* by A. Cunningham.
D.H.N.I. : *The Dynastic History of Northern India* by H.C. Ray.
E. & D. : *The History of India as told by its own Historians* by H.M. Elliot and J. Dowson.
E.I. : *Epigraphia Indica.*
P.C. : *Prabodha Candrodaya.*
P.C.M. : *Prabandha Cintāmani.*
P.R. : *Paramāla Rāso.*
Pr. R. : *Prithvīraja Rāso.*
P.R.A.S.W.C. : *Progress Report of the Archaeological Survey of India,* Western Circle.
R.A.T.T. : *Rāstrakūtas and Their Times* by A.S. Altekar.
R.T. : *Rājatarangini.*
Sachau : *Alberuni's India* by E.C. Sachau.
T.A. (D.) : *Tabqat-i-Akbari,* Tr. by B. De.
T.C.C.P.I. : *Tribes and Castes of the Central Provinces of India* by R.V. Russel.
T.F. (B.) : *Tarikh-i-Firishta,* Tr. by J. Briggs.
T.K. : *Al-Tarikhul-Kamil,* Bulak, Vol. IX.
T.N. (R.) : *Tabaqat-i-Nasiri,* Tr. by H.G. Raverty.
T.P. : *The Paramârs* by P. Bhatia.

List of Illustrations

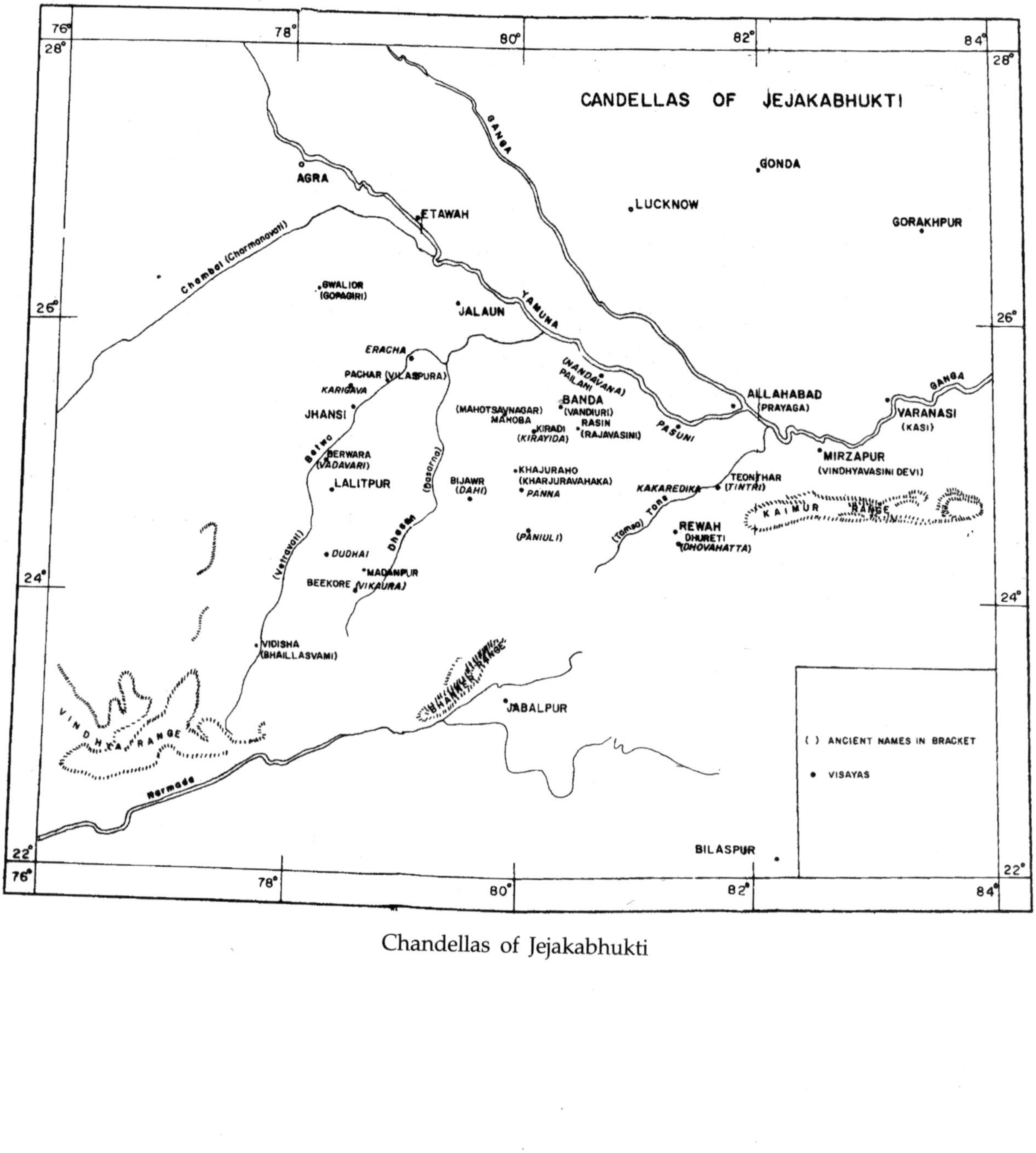

Chandellas of Jejakabhukti

Introduction

SIGNIFICANCE OF THE TOPIC

The Chandellas of Jejakabhukti occupy a significant place both in the political and cultural history of India. They adorned their kingdom with forts, palaces, temples, lakes and tanks, which were chiefly centred in their strongholds of Mahoba (ancient Mahotsvanagar), Kalanjara and Ajaigarh (Jayapura-durga)[1] and to a lesser degree, in their towns of Dudhai, Chandpur, Madanpur and Deogarh. But none of these places could be compared in magnificence with Khajuraho, which was decorated by the Chandellas with tanks and temples. According to literary tradition, the place originally had eighty-five temples but at present only twenty-five remain in different stages of preservation. Recently, a large and beautiful temple was unearthed in the southern area of the site.[2] Thus, the contribution of the Chandellas in the field of art and architecture is much more significant than their political achievements.

Khajuraho is surrounded by the hilly mountain ranges of the Vindhyas. A small stream flows nearby and the wild natural growth tends to add on to the scenic beauty of the place. The neighbouring hills supplied the artists with massive slabs of stones needed for the construction of huge temples, which are built entirely of sandstone.

According to the *Visnudharmottar Purana*,[3] "consecrated images should be installed in forts, auspicious cities, at the head of shop-lined streets or in villages or in hamlets of cowherds. At river-sides in the forests, gardens, at sides of ponds, on hill tops, in beautiful valleys and particularly in caves. The images should be installed because, in these places, the 'denizens of heaven' are not present. In places without tanks, gods are not present; therefore, a temple should not be built in a place having no tank on the right, the left or in front. A temple built on an island is considered to be auspicious".[4] The Chandellas followed these instructions in their art and architecture. Thus, the natural surroundings played a very significant role in Chandella art and architecture.

Much work has been done on Chandella art and architecture by Cunningham, Havell, Fergusson, Percy Brown, Stella Kramrisch, Zannas, Krishna Deva, Vidya Prakash, Urmila

Agrawal, Devangana Desai and others, but no systematic analysis of the material content of art and architecture pertaining to environmental aspect has been made so far.

The Jejakabhukti is a beautiful region with rich flora and fauna that is set against a lovely and picturesque landscape. The high mountains, the flowing rivers, the water-falls, the fecund forests, the trees with their coat of green and variegated flowers, most of them spreading an aroma of perfume all round, the colourful animals whose every little movement suggests their habits and propensities, the birds warbling sweet songs, even the butterflies with tinted patterns on their wing hopping on every flower to sip nectar therefrom, have all been a joy and an inspiration for the artists during the Chandella period.

Before studying the environment in Chandella art and architecture, we must know the region over which the Chandellas ruled and where monuments were constructed during the period concerned. The boundaries of Chandella kingdom varied from time to time but the area roughly corresponded to what is now known as Bundelkhand. At the climax of the Chandella power in the eleventh century AD, this region was bound on all four sides by rivers – in the north by the Yamuna, in the south by the Narmada, in the east the Tamasa, and in the west the Chambal.[5] The tract was known during sixth century BC as Chedi,[6] during the Chandella times as Jejakabhukti,[7] and since the fourteenth century as Bundelkhand.[8] During ancient times, the region played a glorious role in the political and cultural history of India. According to local tradition, the *ashrama*s of famous *rishi*s like Valmiki, Vedavyasa, Atri and Agastya were located here.[9] This region is also known for its numerous lakes, formed by erecting embarkments across the streams. The region is rich in natural resources, and being traversed by many branches of the Vindhyas and numerous rivers and rivulets, it is remarkable for its natural beauty which even attracted the attention of Rama.[10] Thus, geographical and environmental features influenced the physical and mental activities of the people of the concerned area. The mountains, rivers, and its distinctive fauna and flora are also reflected in the Chandella art and architecture. The numerous art motifs, decorative patterns and designs are taken from the natural surroundings of the region. The rocks of the region provided artists the material for construction of temples, caves, tanks and sculptures. Similarly, the quarries of Panna provided a very finely grained sandstone ranging from a creamy buff to a deep golden hue for the construction of temples and sculptures at Khajuraho. The texture and colour of the stone gave warmth and fullness to the modelled surface. It is smooth where the stone is not weathered. Evenness of surface texture is one of the qualities on which the Indian craftsman insists throughout.[11] A panel kept in the Khajuraho museum depicts a huge number of labourers carrying stones with the help of a long wooden pole.[12] The diamond mines at Panna equally add to the ruler's richness to construct high profile temples at Khajuraho and in other art centres. The environmental factor plays a very significant role in the study of art and architecture of the Chandellas, which is least studied by the scholars so far.

SOURCES

The Chandellas of Jejakabhukti were one of the most important dynasties of India during early medieval India. In fact, nothing was known of the dynasty until the publication of Cunningham's *Archaeological Survey Reports*. The importance of these reports and the significant contribution of Cunningham can be assessed by the fact that even today no study of the Chandellas is possible without the help of his Reports, and many conclusions made by Cunningham still stand to this day. He made an attempt to write the history of the dynasty for the first time based on the material available to him. Smith wrote an article on the Chandellas in

1908, in Volume XXXVIL of *Indian Antiquity*. Kielhorn published many important inscriptions of the Chandella dynasty, which throw significant light on the Chandella history.

The sources of the Chandella history may mainly be divided into two parts – literary and archaeological – which are either indigenous or foreign. First, we will take up the former.

1. Literary Sources

The material for the study of the Chandella history lies scattered in a variety of Sanskrit, Prakrita and Apabhransa works – epics, dramas, minor poems, law digests, religious literature, social satire, anthologies and miscellaneous works including those on practical arts, in the accounts of foreign travellers.

However, here we are mainly concerned with contemporary sources related to Chandella history. Further, with a view to a proper assessment of the development of environmental aspect of the Chandella period, the relevant sources of the earlier period have been examined. Similarly, the works composed later, which reflect the atmosphere of the early period, have also been utilised.

The following works of early medieval period give us valuable information regarding the history of the Chandellas:

(i) The Rajatarangini of Kalhan

Kalhan, the famous Kashmiri poet, flourished in the middle of the twelfth century. He gives in the *Rajatarangini* a chronology of the kings of Kashmir, right from the beginning to his own days. A Brahmin by birth and devoted to Shiva, he was free from the narrow sectarian outlook. From his work it appears that he had carefully studied the epics, the works of classical authors and earlier historians, and many other sciences. As a basis for his excellent *Rajatarangini*, Kalhan seems to have used the works of early chroniclers in the field, and also gathered first-hand information from copper-plates, various eulogies, and family records.[13] The work is unique as the only known "attempt to true history in the whole of surviving Sanskrit literature".[14] Though the work of Kalhan is related to the history of Kashmir, it also gives very significant information regarding the contemporary history of India. Thus, *Rajatarangini* is an important source for the history of the Chandellas.

(ii) The Prabodha Chandrodaya of Krishna Misra

The *Prabodha Chandrodaya* of Krishna Misra is an allegory in six acts in defence of the Advaita Vaishnava doctrine. This was written to commemorate the victory of the Chandella king Kirtivarman over the Kalachuris. He gives the credit for this victory to Gopala, an ally of Kirtivarman, whereas the epigraphs give all the credit to the king himself.[15] There are several passages in the drama which throw light on this historical event. At one place, Gopala is compared to Maha Varaha who "raised up the earth when it had sunk in the waters of destructions". Elsewhere, he is said to have, like Parasurama, extirpated the race of tyrannical kings, or to have ripped asunder, like Narasimha, the breasts of the powerful enemies.[16] Thus, the *Prabodha Chandrodaya* is an important source of Chandella history. It also gives information of the cultural life during the time of the Chandellas.

(iii) The Rupakasatakam of Vatsraja

Vatsraja, who served as minister under Paramardideva and Trailokyavarman, was the writer of six dramas. Following are the six plays of Vatsraja:

a. *Kiratarjuniya* (Vyā yoga)
b. *Karpuracharita* (Bhana)
c. *Hasyachudamani* (Farce)
d. *Rukmini-haran* (Ihamrga)
e. *Tripuradha* (Dima)
f. *Samudramanthana* (Samavkara)

These dramas of Vatsraja give valuable information of Chandella society and economy. We find in them a realistic picture of the contemporary period. R.K. Dikshit utilised the material of Vatsraja in his book *Chandellas of Jejakabhukti and their times*.[17] These dramas also give information regarding the contemporary environment. Thus, the dramas of Vatsraja are a significant source for the study of Chandella history.

(iv) The Prithviraja Raso

The bardic literature of Chandrabardayi, the *Prithviraja Raso,* is significant for the study of Chandella-Chamana conflict. The main story of *Prithviraja Raso* is well known. This work gives significant information regarding the victory of Prithviraja over the Chandella ruler, Paramardideva. This is also confirmed by the inscription.[18]

(v) The Lay of Alha

The 'Lay of Alha' is very popular in the Bundelkhand region. It is also very interesting, and has been translated into English ballad metre by V. Waterfield, and published with an introduction by George Grierson on the historical background and the importance of the work. The 'Lay of Alha' painted Alha and Udal as great heroes of their times. They fought bravely with the armies of Prithviraja Chamana. They were famous for their heroic performances during the time of Parmaradideva. The 'Alahakhand' is very popular in the folk culture of Bundelkhand. There is at least some truth behind the stories that Parmaradideva could not face boldly the attack of Prithviraja Chamana. 'Alha' was written by Jagnaik.

(vi) The Parmal Raso (Mahobakhand)

The 'Mahobakhand' is generally taken to be a part of the *Prithviraja Raso* of the bard Chandrabardayi.[19] The question of the authorship of the 'Mahobakhand' is a matter of controversy. Shyam Sunder Das, who edited the text under the caption *Parmal Raso* concluded that its authorship cannot be ascribed to Chandrabardayi.[20] He suggested that it would not be unnatural for a Bundelkhand poet to compose the 'Raso' (Mahobakhand) on the lines of either Chandrabardayi's story or Jagnaik Rai's 'Alha Raso', or similar other works and incorporate in it the material derived from traditions.[21] According to Shyam Sunder Das, the extant 'Mahobakhand' could not have been composed earlier than the 17th or 18th century of Vikram Era, i.e., much later in point of time than the *Prithviraja Raso* of Chandrabardayi, who was a friend and contemporary of Prithviraja Chamana.[22]

The first chapter of the 'Mahobakhand' relates the story of the birth of Chandra Varman [Chandra Brahma (Varman) Utpattikhand], who is described as the first ruler of the Chandella dynasty. While describing the birth of the prince of Chandella lineage, the author introduces the story of Hemavati, the daughter of Hemaraja, a priest of the Gahirawars, and her union with the Moon God.[23] Reference to the story has already been made by Cunningham[24] and H.C. Ray.[25] The story has been rejected as a 'silly legend' by V.A. Smith.[26] But a critical study of the legend may reveal, in spite of its apparent absurdities, a substratum of fact.[27] The information regarding the number of temples constructed at Khajuraho is more or less correct and confirmed by the explorations of the Archaeological Survey of India. Thus, in spite of shortcomings, this work gives some important information regarding the Chandella dynasty.

(vii) Works of Bhoja Parmara

Bhoja Parmara was a great ruler of the Parmara dynasty. He was a contemprorary of the Chandella king, Vidyadhara. He has composed many works on different subjects. The *Yuktikalpataru*, a work on state-craft, and *Samrangana-Sutradhar*, a work on architecture,[27] yield some valuable information regarding the contemporary life.

(viii) The Aparajita-Pracha of Bhuvan Deo

The *Aparajita-Pracha* is a work on architecture which was composed in the twelfth century AD.[29] It gives valuable information on study of the Chandella art and architecture.

(ix) The Sukti-muktavali by Jalhana

The *Sukti-muktavali* gives important information regarding the history of Kalanjara, which was an important fort of the Chandellas and played a significant role in protecting the kingdom. The *Sukti-muktavali* mentions a king of Kalanjara named Bhimata, who composed five dramas of which *Swapanadarsana* was considered the best.[30] The Kasia stone inscription[31] of Kalachuris of Sarayupara mentions two Kalachuri princes bearing the same name.[32] Thus, this work gives significant information regarding the literary contribution of the Kalachuri king, Bhimata I.[33]

(x) The Sukraniti of Sukra

Being a broad-based 'niti' work, the *Sukraniti* would have much valuable work from the point of view of studying the polity of the Chandellas. The date is highly controversial. Gustav Oppert who edited the text ascribes it to the fourth century AD.[34] B.K. Sarkar[35] also supported the same view. V.S. Agrawal considers it to be Kautilya's *Arthsastra* of the Gupta period.[35] K.P. Jaiswal[37] and A.S. Altekar[37] placed it in the eighth century AD. Rajendra Lal Mitra,[38] on the other hand, held that the work could not have been older than the sixteenth century AD. The mention of gun and gun-powder in it led Keith[40] also to assign it to the later medieval period. Some[38] even regard it as a nineteenth century text on the basis of evidence which deserves consideration. After examining carefully the material evidence of the text, it can hardly be denied that it contains traditions of more than one period and some of them belong to early medieval period as well.[41] It gives reference to the prevalence of tantrism and also condemns it. Thus, *Sukraniti* is important for the study of the administrative system of the Chandellas.

2. Foreign Accounts

Indigenous sources can be supported by foreign accounts. Among the accounts of Chinese travellers, mention may be made of Hiuen Tsang who visited India during the time of Harshavardhan. He gives an account of the political, social, economic and religious condition of India during the seventh century AD. Some of the scholars have identified Jejakabhukti (Jihoti) with Chi-Chi-to (Watters) or Chi-ki-to (Beal) mentioned by Hiuen Tsang, in this regard of the unequivocal statement of the Mahoba inscription.[42] According to the Chinese traveller Chih-Chi-to lay more than 1000 *li* in circuit, the soil was rich, the crops were abundant, and pulse and wheat were the chief products. The majority of the people were not Buddhists, but there were some tens of monasteries with a few brethren of other systems. The king, who was a Brahmin, was a firm believer in Buddhism, and encouraged men of merit and learned scholars of other lands to collect here.[43] The description is so indefinite that little can be made out of it in determination of the identity of the province or its capital.[44]

Among the accounts of foreign travellers, Al Beruni's *India* (11th century AD) figures most prominently. This work is of singular importance for the study of the social, economic and cultural history of the early medieval period. The Arab traveller has written at length about the customs, beliefs, literature, learning and environment of India during the time of his visit. His outlook all along has been fairly objective. He gives account of the Chandellas and their capital. His information is also useful to study the contemporary environment of the Chandella period.

The accounts of the other Arab traveller Ibn Battuta, who visited Khajuraho in the year 1335, mentioned the *jogis* and their magic. In his memoirs, he describes a large pond, one mile in length, surrounded by tall temples. This must be the Shivasagar tank near the western group of temples.[43] Following some other works of Arabic and Persian of early and later medieval period also gives us valuable information for the study of the Chandella history:

a. Al Badaoni – *Muntakhab-ul-Tawarikh.*
b. Al Beruni – *Tahquiqi ma Lil-Hind.*
c. Al Gardizi – *Kitab Zaimul Akhbar.*
d. Al Utbi – *Tarikh-i-Yamini.*
e. Hasan Nizami – *Taj-ul-Maasir.*
f. Ibn-ul-Athir – *Al-Tarikh-ul Kamil.*
g. Minhaj-us-Siraj – *Tabaqat-Nasiri.*
h. Muhammad – *Tarikh-i-Firishta.*
i. Nizam-ud-Din – *Tabaqat-Akbari.*

The above books are useful for the study of Chandella history.

3. Archaeological Sources

The archaeological sources related to Chandella history may be divided into three parts:

(i) Coins
(ii) Inscriptions
(iii) Monuments

(i) Coins

Coins are an important source of the Chandella history. They provide significant information regarding the socio-economic condition of the Chandella period. The coins of the Chandella dynasty are available from the middle of eleventh century AD. It is supposed that no coin of such powerful rulers as Dhanga and Vidyadhara are known. The coinage of the Chandella dynasty starts with the reign of Kirtivarman (c. AD 1060-1100) and continues up to the reign of Viravarman (c. 1250-1286). The coins of Kirtivarman, which are almost exact copies of the coins of Gangeyadeva, are important evidence of the success of the Kalachuris.

The largest number of available Chandella coins belong to Madanavarman. These may be classified according to their denomination. Thus, coins give us significant information regarding the Chandella dynasty. Coins played an important role for the reconstruction of the Chandella history.

(ii) Inscriptions

Far more important than coins are inscriptions. The Chandella rulers issued more than seventy inscriptions. Some of these were engraved on the surface of rocks, on walls of the temples, on pillars forming part of structures or on slabs of stone. Others were on copper plates. These were the Charters of land grants. These inscriptions were records of installation of temples or images, works of public utility, like gardens, wells, embarkments, platforms and other forms of structures. The inscriptions have served as a main source of political, social, economic and religious history of the Chandellas. Inscriptions give information about the construction of temples, images, forts, gardens, tanks and other such activities. Thus, inscriptions are a valuable source for the study of Chandella art and architecture. S.K. Mitra and others utilised the epigraphical material for writing the history of the Chandellas.[45]

(iii) Monuments

The Chandellas were great builders. They decorated their kingdom with forts, palaces, temples, lakes and tanks, which were mainly centred at Ajaigarh, Kalanjara, Mahoba, Khajuraho and other places of their kingdom. During their time, Khajuraho was the main centre of temples. These monuments, which were constructed during the Chandella period, reveal the various aspects of cultural life. They are a valuable source for the study of the origin and development of art and architecture during the Chandella period.

REVIEW OF THE WORK ALREADY DONE

The review of the Chandella historiography provides a basis to study the trends of Chandella art and architecture. The study of the Chandella history began during the nineteenth century. Lieutenant William Price presented a paper in 1813 at the *Journal of Asiatic Society of Bengal* on the Sanskrit inscription found at Mau near Khajuraho,[46] which for the first time drew the attention of the historians to the Chandella dynasty. Captain T.S. Burt,[47] who visited Khajuraho in 1838, was struck by the sculptural and architectural beauty of the surviving temples. He briefly described the Visvanatha, Nandi, Lakshmana Varaha and Matangeshwara temples, of which the last one was in active worship and copied Dhanga's stone inscription dated AD 1002. Thus, the credit of rediscovering Khajuraho goes to T.S. Burt. Captain W.R. Pogson[48] published his book, *History of Bundelas* in the year 1828, in which he mentioned some important places related to the Chandella history and art with maps and description of Kalanjara and Ajaigarh. General F.C. Maisy[49] had published his paper along with line drawings, maps and inscriptions in the *Journal of Asiatic Society of Bengal* in 1848, entitled *Description of the Antiquities at Kalinjar* in which he has given a very extensive description of the Chandella fort at Kalanjara. Along with Kalanjara fort, he has given a brief account of another Chandella fort at Ajaigarh. In 1852 he made the earliest line drawing of Khajuraho temples.[50] Actually there was nothing authentic known of the Chandella dynasty until the publication of Cunningham's *Archaeological Survey Reports* (Vols. II, VII, X and XXI) in the years 1864 to 1885.[51] The significance of the Reports and contribution of Cunningham can be measured by the fact that even today no study of the Chandellas is possible without the help of his Reports and many of the conclusions drawn by Cunningham still hold good. On the basis of the Reports and other inscriptions, Smith published a scholarly paper on the Chandellas in the year 1908, in Volume XXXVII of *Indian Antiquary*.[52]

Till this time the history of the Chandellas and other dynasties was still very obscure and little of the period was known until the publication in 1931 and 1936 of H.C. Ray's *Dynastic History of Northern India,* which not only contributed to the knowledge of the history of dynasties, but also emphasized the vast scope of the subject and need for future research.[53] Gorelal Tiwari published his book entitled *Bundelkhand Ka Itihas* in Hindi in 1933.[54] His book gives a brief history of Bundelkhand region. Keshav Chandra Mishra's book, entitled *Chandella*

Aur Unka Rajatava Kala, was published in 1954 in Hindi.[55] He studied the Chandella history, culture and art on the basis of literary and archaeological sources. The first research work on Chandella history, entitled *History of the Chandellas,* was published in 1956 by N.S. Bose.[56] He made an attempt to trace the full history of Chandellas on the basis of inscriptions and contemporary literary works. Besides the political history, he has discussed the administration, social, economic, cultural and religious life along with art and architecture during the time of Chandellas in brief. O.C. Gangoly published his monograph called the 'Art of Chandella' in 1957 on the basis of Khajuraho sculptures.[57] This monograph, for the first time, accords aesthetic value to the Chandella sculpture of Khajuraho. In the same year, a special issue of the art journal, *Marg,* on Khajuraho highlighted the sculptural wealth of Khajuraho.[58] In 1958, S.K. Mitra published his doctoral thesis entitled *Early Rulers of Khajuraho,* in which he discussed the political history of the Chandellas and highlighted the socio-economic and religious conditions on the basis of epigraphic sources along with art and architecture of the Chandellas.[59] The second edition of his book was published in 1977 in which he added two appendices, viz., 'Chandella land grants and feudalism,' and 'A Note on the aspect of Chandella architecture'. The former contradicts R.S. Sharma's theory on feudalism and its application to Chandella land grants. The second appendix contains an important suggestion that all the Khajuraho temples, Hindu and Jain, must have been built by the same community of builders, belonging to a single school of architecture, i.e., Nagar style of Central India. As craftsmen they themselves might have had no sectarian bias and represented enthusiastically the requirements of their patrons irrespective of their religious affiliations.[60] Krishna Deva published in 1959 an article in *Ancient India* (No. 15), entitled 'The Temples of Khajuraho in Central India'.[61] In this paper he has studied the Khajuraho sculptures, temple architecture and sculptural art in depth on the basis of site survey and text. He has given a classification of Khajuraho sculptures, which is acceptable to art historians. E. Zannas and J. Aubuyer in 1960 published their work, *Khajuraho.*[62] They gave a detailed description of the temples and their cultural and political background. They have also drawn a vivid picture of the contemporary life lived in the court, in the town and the countryside, the duties, daily routine, and pastimes of the king and the courtiers, rules of battlefield and the marketplace, together with details of prevailing social and religious institutions. They have also assessed the unique place occupied by Khajuraho temples. In the same year Kanwarlal published his book, *Immortal Khajuraho.*[63] This book is written for the tourists. In 1964 Urmila Agrawal published her doctoral dissertation, *Khajuraho Sculptures and their significance.*[64] She made an attempt to study the Khajuraho sculptures on the basis of iconography for the first time. A discussion of the social significance of the sculptures for the study of contemporary social life as revealed in the Khajuraho sculptures was the highlight of this work. The description of female life with reference to her cultural interest in the fine arts, her cosmetics, coiffure, dress and ornaments is a fine analysis, reflecting an essential grasp of the author on extracting cultural data from art and literature. H.D. Sankalia published his paper, 'Socio-economic background of Khajuraho' in the *Journal of Indian History* in 1966.[65] He made an attempt to briefly discuss the factors which made it possible for these magnificent temples to come into existence and which possibly also account for the profoundly erotic elements in its sculptures. The reason for building the temples at Khajuraho seems to him to be that near about Panna, they found not only excellent sandstone but also diamonds.[65] Vidya Prakash published his book, *Cultural life in Khajuraho Sculpture* in 1967.[67] Vidya Prakash's book studies the social life as reflected in sculptures and carving at Khajuraho, and provides both descriptive and pictorial documentation of the contemporary dress and ornaments, hairstyles, cosmetics, dance, music and painting, games and amusements, military life and weapons of war, individual art and profession, furniture and household, education and learning, religious beliefs and traditions, and miscellaneous activities and interprets the erotic themes. In the same year, another book in Hindi titled *Khajuraho Ki Deva Pratimayain* by Ramasraya Awasthi came into print.[68] This was an attempt to study the iconography of some important deities of Khajuraho temples in depth and in which a good textual interpretation of images was brought out. In the meantime, Mulkraj Anand's monograph, *Khajuraho* was published.[69] His attempt was to highlight the aesthetic value of the Khajuraho sculptures. Klaus Bruhn published '*Deogarh*', an important site of Chandella art, in which Jain icons at Deogarh were discussed in detail.[70] Bhagchander Jain published his dissertation, *Deogarh Ki Jain Kala* in which he made an attempt to study the Jain sculptures having iconographic significance found in Deogarh.[71] A.P. Pandey's research work, *Chandella Kalin Bundelkhand Ka Itihas* (1968) in Hindi was a study narrative and its character pertaining to the Chandella art is merely a survey of the Cunningham Reports.[72] In the year 1977, R.K. Dikshit's thesis, *Chandellas of Jejakabhukti* provided an authentic account of the history of the Chandellas and is well documented.[73] It is based on a critical appreciation of the available sources, literary as well as archaeological, and personal explorations leading to the discovery of new inscriptions that had not been noticed earlier. The author has utilised *Rupaksatakam*,[74] an important work of the Chandella times, for the first time – a work that has not been noticed by other writers on the subject. The cultural part of his thesis has remained unpublished till today. K.L. Agrawal's *Khajuraho* in Hindi was released in the year 1980.[75] He made an attempt to study the monuments of Khajuraho in the light of geo-political, socio-economic and religious backgrounds and also added the translation of some important inscriptions of Khajuraho in Hindi. Krishna Deva's guide-book, *Khajuraho* (1966 first edition), published by the Archaeological Survey of India, gives an authentic account of the Khajuraho temples for general readers and also for scholars.[76] One notable monograph by R. Nath published in 1980 is the most comprehensive and well-documented work on the art and architecture of Khajuraho, laying stress on their aesthetic evaluation and interpretation of erotica.[77] S.D. Trivedi's 'Catalogue of Sculptures in the Jhansi Museum,' released in 1983, gives an account of Chandella sculptures found in Jhansi region of Uttar Pradesh.[78] His next publication was *Bundelkhand Ka Puratattava* in Hindi.[79] In this book he described the archaeological sites of the Bundelkhand region and also incorporated some new material found in some sites of Bundelkhand. K.K. Chakravarti released his monograph, 'Khajuraho' in 1985.[80] He had propounded that the Khajuraho artist described the total rather than the partial life of the entire community or of any individual. His sculptures and his temples were the manifestation of his inner vision. The book contains very good photographs and line drawings of the Khajuraho temples and sculptures. Krishna Deva's[81] *Khajuraho* of 1987 contains very good photographs and a new approach towards the study of Khajuraho sculptures and temples. He published again *The Temples of Khajuraho* in two volumes, which is a remarkable work.[82] Krishna Deva contributed a very significant and authentic study of sculptural and architectural study of Chandella art with particular reference to Khajuraho. He has given a scholarly and text-based study of Khajuraho art and architecture. M.N.P. Tiwari's *Khajuraho Ki Jain Puratattava* (1987), in Hindi, provides a critical account of the Jain sculptures of Khajuraho.[83] The author's publication, *Ajaigarh Aur Kalanjara Ki Devapratimayain* (1987) has, for the first time, studied the famous Chandella forts of Ajaigarh and Kalanjara as art centres of the Chandellas.[84] The author brought out the significance of rock-cut Chandella sculptures, which had not been studied by previous art historians of the Chandella school. The sculptures of Ajaigarh and Kalanjara are important from the artistic and iconographic point of view. M.N.P. Tiwari organized a site seminar at Khajuraho in 1987, in which he invited a good number of scholars connected with the subject.[85] It was a good attempt to study the monument at site and discuss the matter of controversy and also exchange views on various aspects related to the sculptural study of the site. The proceedings of the seminar, published by the Department of Archaeology, Madhya Pradesh in 1994, were edited by K.K. Chakravarti, M.N.P. Tiwari and Kamal Giri.[86] It contains papers on different aspects of Khajuraho art and architecture. It is an important contribution by the scholars in the field of Chandella art and architecture. Devangana Desai has made a genuine contribution to the study of Chandella art and iconography.[87] She has published many research papers on various aspects of Khajuraho art in Indian and foreign journals and also brought out her book, *The Religious Imagery of Khajuraho,* in which she discusses critically the importance of religious imagery of Khajuraho and placement of the images. Her contributions are commendable and an original attempt has been made to explain the meaning of erotic sculpture on the textual basis. She propounded the view that erotic sculptures are not the only attraction of Khajuraho. She has also discussed the religious trends of Khajuraho prevalent during the Chandella period and their impact on the art and architecture of Khajuraho. Another book, entitled *Khajuraho,* was released by her in 2000.[88] This book is very useful for scholars as well as for general visitors to Khajuraho. In this book she has incorporated latest information regarding the temples of Khajuraho. P.K. Mishra[89] published *Khajuraho* in 2001, with the latest discoveries of a new temple at Khajuraho. The excavation of the Bijamandal mound is an important discovery. It has exposed the plinth of the largest temple at Khajuraho, longer than that of the ground Kanderiya Mahadeva. Mishra has also furnished a detailed history of the conservation work these monuments have already undergone and such further measures proposed to be undertaken for them.

For the study of Chandella history and art, I have made an attempt to incorporate all the significant publications related to the historiography of the Chandellas. The review of the work gives us an idea about the direction of studies done so far on the subject concerned. We can conclude that most studies on Chandella art are focused around Khajuraho.

NOTES AND REFERENCES

1. *Epigraphia Indica,* Vol. I, pp. 325-30.
2. Devangana Desai, *Khajuraho,* p. 6.
3. *Visnudharmottar Purana,* Part III, Chapter- XCIII, pp. 25-31.
4. Urmila Agrawal, *Khajuraho Sculptures and their Significance,* p. 5.
5. Devangana Desai, *Khajuraho,* p. 8; R.K. Dikshit, *Chandellas of Jejakabhukti,* pp. 10-11.
6. *Journal of the Asiatic Society of Bengal* (1895), p. 253.
7. *Epigraphia Indica,* Vol. I, p. 40.
8. R.K. Dikshit, *op. cit.,* p. 12, fn. 13.
9. *Ibid.,* p. 11; Devangana Desai, *The Religious Imagery of Khajuraho,* p. 38.
10. *Ramayana* (Gita Press), II, 94.
11. Stella Kramrisch, *J.I.S.O.A.,* Vol. I, pp. 102-03.
12. *Journal of Indian History,* No. 136, p. 34, fn. 2.
13. R.C. Majumdar (ed.), *The Struggle for Empire,* p. 308.
14. A.L. Basham (ed.), *The Historians of India, Pakishtan and Ceylon,* p. 58.
15. R.K. Dikshit, *op. cit.,* p. 103, fn. 2.
16. *Epigraphia,* Vol. I, pp. 219-22, Vs. 26.
17. R.K. Dikshit, *op. cit.,* Preface, p. vii.
18. N.S. Bose, *History of Chandellas,* p. 188.
19. S.K. Mitra, *The Early Rulers of Khajuraho,* p. 14.
20. *Ibid.*
21. *Ibid.*

22. *Prithviraj Raso*, Introduction, p. 2.
23. S.K. Mitra, *op. cit.*, p. 14.
24. *A.S.I.R.*, Vol. II, pp. 445-46.
25. H.C. Ray, *Dynastic History of Northern India*, Vol. II, p. 665.
26. *Indian Antiquary*, Vol. XXXVII, pp. 136-37.
27. S.K. Mitra, *op. cit.*, p. 15.
28. B.N.S. Yadav, *Society and Culture in Northern India*, Introduction, p. xiii.
29. *Ibid.*
30. *Suktimuktavali*, p. 16.
31. *Epigraphia Indica*, Vol. XVIII, pp. 128-37.
32. S.K. Sullerey, Prof. A. Awasthi, Vol. pp. 40-41.
33. *Ibid.*
34. *Sukraniti*, Introduction, p. viii.
35. B.K. Sarkar, *Positive Background of Hindu Sociology*, BK II, part I, pp. 63, 71.
36. V.S. Agrawal, *Harshacharit Ek Sanskritik Adhyayana*, p. 219.
37. Beni Prasad, *State in Ancient India*, p. 466, fn. 1.
38. A.S. Altekar, *State and Government in Ancient India*, p. 12.
39. B.N.S. Yadev, *op. cit.*, Introduction, p. xv.
40. *A History of Sanskrit Literature*, p. 464.
41. B.N.S. Yadev, *op. cit.*, Introduction, p. xv.
42. *Indian Antiquary*, Vol. XXXVII, p. 131.
43. Watters, *On Yuan Chwang's Travels in India*, II, p. 251.
44. R.K. Dikshit, *op. cit.*, p. 13.
45. S.K. Mitra, *op. cit.*
46. *Asiatic Researches*, Vol. 12, 1818, pp. 360-69; O.P. Kejariwal, *Journal of Asiatic Society of Bengal and the Discovery of India's Past*, pp. 114-15.
47. *Journal of Asiatic Society of Bengal*, Vol. VIII, 1839.
48. W.R. Pogson, *History of the Bundelas*, Calcutta, 1828.
49. F.C. Maisy, *Journal of Asiatic Society of Bengal*, Vol. VII, 1848.
50. Devangana Desai, *Khajuraho*, p. 4, Fig. 1.
51. A. Cunningham, *Archaeological Survey of India Reports*, 1864-1885, Vols. II, VII, X, XXI, Calcutta, 1871-1887.
52. *Indian Antiquary*, Vol. XXXVII, 1908.
53. H.C. Ray, *op. cit.*, Calcutta, 1931-1936.
54. Gorelal Tiwari, *Bundelkhand Ka Ithasa*, Allahabad, 1933.
55. Keshav Chandra Mishra, *Chandella Aur Unka Rajatavakala*, Varanasi, 1954.
56. N.S. Bose, *op. cit.*, Calcutta, 1956.
57. O.C. Gangoly, *The Art of the Chandellas*, Calcutta, 1957.
58. Mulk Raj Anand, *Marg*, Bombay.
59. S.K. Mitra, *op. cit.*, 1958.
60. *Ibid.*, 1977, Second Edition.
61. Krishna Deva, *Temples of Khajuraho in Central India*, No. 15, 1958.
62. E. Zannas and J. Anboyer, *Khajuraho*, 1958.
63. Kanwarlal, *Immortal Khajuraho*, Delhi, 1965.
64. Urmila Agrawal, *Khajuraho Sculptures and their Significance*, Delhi, 1964.
65. H.D. Sankalia, 'Socio-Economic Background of Khajuraho', *Journal of Indian History*, No. 136, 1966, pp. 29-42.
66. *Ibid.*, p. 34.
67. Vidya Prakash, *Khajuraho – A Study of the Cultural Conditions of Chandella's Society*, Bombay, 1967.
68. Ramasaraya Awasthi, *Khajuraho Ki Deva Pratimanyain*, Agra, 1967.
69. Mulkraj Anand, *Khajuraho*, Bombay, 1968.
70. Bruhn Klaus, *The Jain Images of Deogarh*, Leiden, 1969.

71. Bhagchandra Jain, *Deogarh Ki Jainkala*, Delhi, 1974.
72. A.P. Pandey, *Chandella Kalin Bundelkhand Ka Itihasa*, Allahabad, 1968.
73. R.K. Dikshit, *Chandellas of Jejakabhukti*, Delhi, 1977.
74. Vatsraj, *Rupakasatakam*, Bombay, 1918.
75. K.L. Agrawal, *Khajuraho*, Delhi, 1980.
76. Krishna Deva, *Khajuraho*, Delhi, 1977, (Fifth Edition).
77. R. Nath, *The Art of Khajuraho*, Delhi, 1980.
78. S.D. Trivedi, *Catalogue of Sculptures in Jhansi Museum*, 1983.
79. S.D. Trivedi, *Bundelkhand Ka Puratattava*, Jhansi, 1984.
80. K.K. Chakravarti, *Khajuraho*, Delhi, 1985.
81. Krishna Deva, *Khajuraho* (Brajbasi), Delhi, 1987.
82. Krishna Deva, *Temples of Khajuraho*, (two vols.), Delhi, 1990.
83. M.N.P. Tiwari, *Khajuraho Ka Jain Puratattava*, Varanasi, 1987.
84. S.K. Sullerey, *Ajaigarh Aur Kalanjara Ki Devapratimayain*, Delhi, 1987.
85. M.N.P. Tiwari, *Organise U.G.C. Seminar at Khajuraho*, 1987.
86. Chakravarti, M.N.P. Tiwari and Girikamal (eds.), *Khajuraho in Perspective*, Bhopal, 1994.
87. Devangana Desai, *The Religious Imagery of Khajuraho*, Mumbai, 1966.
88. Devangana Desai, *Khajuraho*, Delhi, 2000.
89. P.K. Mishra, *Khajuraho*, Delhi, 2001.

1

Geographical and Historical Background of Chandella Art and Architecture

GEOGRAPHICAL BACKGROUND

The art and culture of a country or region are, to a great extent, governed by their geographical features. As Febvre remarked, "It is the whole life of man, not only their political life, it is the whole of their institutions, and above all, but not exclusively, their economic organisation which are in close relation with the environment."[1] It is therefore essential that history of any particular place or period must be constructed upon the physical factors which played an immense part in its final making. Hence, the significance of geography and its relation with history can in no way be minimised.

The study of environment is of great importance so is its relevance on man's creativity. Jejakabhukti, owing to its unique geographical location between the northern and southern part of India, its hilly surroundings and its natural resources, has attracted kings and sages alike through all the ages. It was a link between the north and south used by invaders, merchants, caravan of traders and religious missionaries. This strange natural phenomenon, though catastrophic to some extent, made people sturdy, self-sufficient and God fearing. This is why we find Jejakabhukti blessed with huge cultural remains well marked in quality as well as variety. The geographical configuration largely influenced the history and creativity of the Chandellas.

The topography of Jejakabhukti presents a contrast of plains and hills, and rivers and forests. Indeed, the beauty of the region is due to the richness of this variation. The region is divided into two parts, the southern consisting of hills divided into hill ranges and the north sloping down to the plains south of Yamuna. The tract is apparently a level plain gradually widening from the south to north towards Yamuna. In the south it is approached by hills which have been divided geographically into three ranges, viz., the Vindhyachal to the north-east, the Panna range to the south, and Bhandair range to the south-west. The Vindhyachal range, which in no place exceeds 2000 feet[2] above sea-level, commences near Sihonda on the river Sindh, proceeding south-west to Narwar, then south-east, and thence north-east to Ajaigarh and Kalanjara and further east Bargadh where it crosses the limits of Jejakabhukti. Its lower parts are formed of granite, which is overlaid by sandstone and sometimes by trap of volcanic origin. The Panna range rises to the south of the plateau of Vindhyachal hills. The primary rock is overlaid by a thick bed of sandstone, which is itself in some places covered by the volcanic trap. The third or Bhandair range, which rises in the south-west of Panna range, is generally formed of sandstone.

Spate has correctly described the region thus:

> Jejakabhukti (Bundelkhand) is recognisable by a mass of rounded hummocky hills, with almost a roches moutonnées effect, typical tropical exfoliation weathering in the reddish Bundelkhand (Jejakabhukti) – Gneiss, cut across by innumerable white quastizite dykes, in all sizes from veins of a few inches to massive walls. The frequent construction of drainage by the dykes favours a multiplicity of small half natural, half artificial tanks and so enables agriculture to be carried on with some security in a region of variable rainfall around forty five inches.[3]

From these hills, a number of rivers flow north or north-east towards the Yamuna, of which the most important is the Betwa; there are a number of minor rivers in the region, viz., the Pahuj, the Jamani, the Birma, the Bhagain and the Paisuni.

The rivers and hill ranges divide this region of Central India into separate parts with differing physical characteristics, as following:

(1) Between the Sindhu (Sindh) and Dhasan lies the first part of Bundelkhand, which includes the valley of the Betwa, one of the important rivers of northern India. It rises in Bhopal and flows in the north-easterly direction to meet the Yamuna near the Hamirpur district of Uttar Pradesh. The Dhasan itself is one of the tributaries.[4] The Pahuj is also in this area, rising near Datia and meeting the Sindh a few miles before the latter's confluence with the Yamuna, and the Jamni is a small tributary of the Betwa meeting the latter near Orchha.

(2) The stretch of region between the Dhasan and the Ken (Karnavati) rivers formerly comprised districts of Panna and Chattarpur of Madhya Pradesh and Hamirpur district of Uttar Pradesh and adjoining areas. Immediately after the Ken rises the Panna range, which traverses right across Jejakabhukti. Below the Ken near its confluence with the Yamuna, but to the north of Panna range, is located the Banda district of Uttar Pradesh which should also come in this group. It is watered by the small river named Baghain, which pours itself into the Yamuna. This river surrounds the famous Chandella fort of Kalanjara.

(3) Between the Panna range and the Kaimur, there is a low-lying tract, generally sloping towards the Gangetic basin.[5] The eastern portion is watered by the river Tons, rising from the Kaimur hill to the south of Maihar. Further below are the districts of Damoh and Sagar of Madhya Pradesh bounded on the south by the hill range known as Bhander. Below the Kaimur is the Son, which rises from the Amarkantaka in Madhya Pradesh, flows north and turns right only from the base of the Kaimur.

There are dense forests in the west, south and south-eastern parts of Jejakabhukti, while the northern parts are covered by areas of brush country due to the decline in rainfall, though the surroundings contain ancient centres of habitation; the ancient forests had been destroyed by man and have been replaced by the secondary scrubs.[6] Bamboos of good quality are exported from Ajaigarh and Kalanjara. *Tendu* and *mahuas* are good trees in the Jejakabhukti. There are also teak forests in this region. The fauna of the forests includes tiger, bear, panther, leopard, wolf, hyena, antelope, deer, fox monkeys, etc.[7]

Jejakabhukti has extensive mineral resources. Panna is famous for its diamond mines. Iron-ore of good quality is found in the Banda and Jhansi districts. Limestone and stone for building purpose are exported to the other parts of the country. The Chandellas used the stone for building their temples at Khajuraho and other places of their kingdom.[8]

The climate of the region is hot and rain is moderate. The climate of the year is divided into three main seasons, viz., winter (October to February), summer (March to May), and rains (June to September). Agriculture, the main profession of the people, largely depends upon the monsoon rains which give a variable rainfall, around 45 inches, although lakes, tanks and reserviors also had been constructed for irrigation purposes by the Chandellas. The most fertile soil of Jejakabhukti is known as Regur or Mar, medium light black in colour. Wheat, barley, gram, mustard, rice, maize, jawar, bajra, pulses and cotton are the main crops which are harvested twice in the year in autumn (*kharif*) and spring (*rabi*).

The geographical position of the Chandella kingdom was further strengthened by the possession of the important and almost inaccessible forts of Ajaigarh, Kalanjara and Mahoba. The importance of these forts to the Chandella kingdom is clearly evident from the history of the dynasty. The whole history of the Chandellas has centred round the strongest fort of Kalanjara and to a lesser degree, the fort of Ajaigarh. Time and again the fortune of the dynasty depended on the possession of Kalanjara.[9] The extraordinary importance of forts in the Chandella state was due to the geographical situation of the country and the method of warfare followed in that period.[10] In spite of all the advantages, the geographical position of the Chandella state had, however, a great disadvantage. It was very difficult for the ruler of such a region to hold up a durable empire, owing to problems of communication and administration of such a hilly region, and the security of the kingdom depended almost entirely on the forts of Kalanjara and Ajaigarh. Once these were taken, the whole region lay open to an invader.[11] Moreover, the hilly tribes of the region often caused trouble in the kingdom, and the reference to the subjugation of the Sabaras, Pulindas and Bhillas in a Chandella inscription,[12] indicates a lack of strong local administration in the outlying areas. The resounding success of the Kalachuris in the last during the reign of Gangeyadeva and Lakshmikarna and the success of Prithviraja Chamana in the west can partially be attributed to the failure of the Chandellas to build up a strong defence on their frontiers.[13]

Thus, the geographical surroundings and environmental conditions influenced the creativity of Chandella artists in various ways and means, and these also reflected in their art and architecture.

HISTORICAL BACKGROUND

The Chandellas of Jejakabhukti ruled over Jejakabhukti for about six centuries[14] out of which at least four hundred years were devoted to the development of art and architecture in their kingdom. The Chandellas, however, are renowned not only for their political achievements but also for their victories of peace. During the rule of the Chandella dynasty either by the rulers themselves or by their chiefs, queens and Jain merchants, temples were built all over the Jejakabhukti region. The Khajuraho group of temples has immortalised them for posterity. Likewise, the large number of masonry works and embarkments have kept alive the memory of Chandella rule in Bundelkhand region.

The origin of the Chandellas, like that of other early medieval dynasties, is obscure and controversial. According to the legend described in the *'Mahobakhand'*, the progenitor of the family was descended from the union of the Moon with Hemavati, the widowed daughter of Hemaraja, the priest of Indrajit, the Gaharawara raja of Kasi.[15] Out of this relationship was born a handsome boy named Chandravarman. Hemavati was worried about the child born out of wedlock, but the Moon god comforted her and prophesied that their son would be the first king of Khajuraho. When he grew up, the Moon god added, he should perform *Bhandya Yajna*, a sacrificial ritual that included among its rites the depiction of erotic figures. He were to also build eighty-five temples at Khajuraho, carved with erotic figures. This would free his mother from the blemish of extramarital love.[16] This is how a seventeeth century legend attempts to account for the large number of temples and their erotic sculptures. The legend also accounts for the mythic origin of the Chandella family.[17]

More than seventy epigraphs of Chandellas, who ruled over Jejakabhukti from circa AD 831 to 1308, have been found. The epigraphs are, however, silent about this story. They trace their ancestry to the mythic sage Chandratreya. The efforts of the Chandella rulers to glorify the origin of the dynasty in the inscriptions is noteworthy in the context of the family's possible tribal associations. Their connection with the tribals has been suggested by many historians, as they worshipped a tribal deity called Maniya-Devi, and had family ties with the Gonds. Like other medieval dynasties, the Chandellas further tried to legitimize their social status by building temples, tanks, and by giving gifts to priestly Brahmanas. Temple-building was emphasized in the medieval *Puranas* as an important religious practice that brought fame and merit to the builder.[17] Apart from Khajuraho, the Chandellas also built temples and tanks at Kalanjara, Ajaigarh, Mahoba, Dudhai, Devagarh, and Madanpur.

Khajuraho was certainly considered a special site and this is where the Chandellas concentrated their temple-building activities. Thus, they converted Khajuraho to a city of temples in Central India. Their earlier temples, built when they were still local rulers and feudatories, were made of rough granite and built on the periphery of the site. Among these are the 'Chausath Yogini' sanctuary for the worship of the sixty-four *yoginis* and the Shiva temple named Lalguan Mahadeva.

1. Nannuka

The Chandella inscription after tracing the origin of the Chandellas from Chandratreya Muni, records the name of Nannuka. He was the first ruler of the Chandella dynasty who is simply called a ruler (*nripa*[18] or *mahipati*[19]), "a touch-stone to test the worth of the gold of the regal order",[20] and "one who playfully decorated the faces of the women of the quarters with the sandal of his fame" (*Yasas candana-kridalauknta dikpurandhri-vadanah*).[21] Another verse describes him as one "whose skill in the use of bows and arrows reminded people of the great Epic hero, Arjuna".[22] Nannuka seems to have ruled over Khajuraho around the beginning of ninth century AD.

2. Vakpati

Nannuka's son and successor was Vakpati. He has been mentioned as the lord of the country, the favourite of his subjects.[23] He must have achieved this fame by granting them freedom from fear by the display of his valour.[24] Besides his military abilities in defeating the enemies in battle, he possessed wisdom and power of speech like his namesake, 'Vakpati'. He is also said to have defeated all his enemies and made the Vindhyas his pleasure mountain.[24] Another epigraph mentions him as a Kshitap and praises him for excelling the mythical king Prithu and Kakustha, in valour and wisdom.[25] He may have somewhat extended the Chandella dominion presumably towards the Vindhyas.

3. Jayasakti and Vijayasakti

Vakpati had two sons, Jayasakti and Vijayasakti. The Khajuraho inscription of AD 954 records

> as the moon and the Kaustobha (arosi) form the ocean of milk, so were born from that home of wonder (Vakpati), two sons Jayasakti and Vijayasakti. Princes, when they are met together, captured praise with shaking of head of the deeds both of them, by the unmeasured power of whose adversaries were destroyed as wood are burnt by blazing fire.[27]

Jayasakti is also described as Jeja and Jejjaka in other inscriptions,[28] while Vijayasakti is mentioned as Vijaya, Vijja and Vija.[29] A fragmentary Mahoba inscription records that "Jayasakti, one of the earlier Chandella rulers, gave his name to Jejabhukti, just as Prithu did to Prithvi."[30] Vijayasakti is also described as having mounted expeditions to the far south to help the cause of an ally who is believed by some scholars to refer to King Devapala of the Pala dynasty, who made an expedition to South India. Subsequently, Jayasakti might have accepted the suzerainty of the Pratihara and won recognised status for his family. H.C. Ray seems quite justified in concluding that Vijayasakti, who succeeded his elder brother Jayasakti as the head of the family, was still a subordinate chief, under the Gurjara, Pratihara, Bhoja or his son Mahendrapala (c. 894-917).[31]

4. Rahila

Rahila was the son and successor of Vijayasakti. The Khajuraho inscription of Dhanga informs us that the younger of the two brothers, i.e., Vijayasakti, begot a son named Rahila, thinking of whom his enemies enjoyed little sleep at night.[32] Another inscription says that he favoured his friends and punished his enemies.[33] The poet Chand ascribes the foundation of the town Rasin in the Banda district of Uttar Pradesh, the full name of which is Rajavasini, to Rahila Varman.[34] Rahila undertook works of public interest, viz., excavation of tanks and lakes and construction of temples, remains of which are still visible at Ajaigarh and Mahoba. At Ajaigarh, a temple bears some stones inscribed with his name,[35] and an old lake with a fine cruciform granite temple on the bank, near Mahoba, is still called 'Rahilya Sagar' after his name.[36]

5. Harsha

The first powerful ruler of the Chandella dynasty was Rahila's son Harsha, who ruled from c. AD 905 to AD 925. The Nanyaura Copper-plate of Dhanga mentions that,

> In the exalted family of the venerable sage Chandratreya the crest jewel of the three worlds, there was a prince, the illustrious Harshadeva (who was) a tree of paradise to those attached (to him), a root of joy to the good, nectar for the eyes of his friends, a mighty combat bodying evil to the host of his enemies, a bridge across the ocean of battle. The prowess of this (prince), who inspired fear by his terrific array of troops (and) who had made tributary (to himself other) sovereigns, was difficult to endure, like the brilliance of the summer sun, which searches with the rays the mountains.[37]

It is evident from this inscription that Harsha was considered as one of the important and powerful rulers of the Chandella dynasty. He reigned at a period when events of great importance were happening on the stage of northern India and the Chandella ruler played no minor part in the affairs of the time. Harsha had matrimonial relations with the Chamanas. The Khajuraho inscription of AD 954 mentions that Harsha married with due rites a suitable (lady) of equal caste, named Kanchuka, sprung from the Chamana family.[38] This matrimonial alliance elevated the social status of the newly rising Chandella family. In the Varanasi Copper-plate inscription of Kalachuri, Karnadeva says that "Kokkalla married a lady named Natta or

Nattadevi, who was born in the Chandella family".[39] These matrimonial alliances with the Kalachuris and the Chamanas undoubtedly increased the social prestige of the Chandellas and helped Harsha to consolidate his position. Harshadeva successfully fought the Rashtrakutas and installed his Pratihara overlord Kshitipala (Mahipala) on the throne of Kanuoj in AD 917. An event that has been recorded was found near the Vamana temple of Khajuraho,[40] the recently excavated brick complex with exquisite stone image of Vamana. Mahishamardini pillars and architectural fragments (now in museum) possibly belong to Harshadeva's time. The pillars have some affinity with the art of the Pratiharas. With Harshadeva can be associated the 'Brahma' (Vishnu) temple on the bank Khajura Sagar.[41] M.A. Dhaky and Krishna Deva suggest that it could be a *Svargarohana-prasada* built in memory of the dead.[42]

6. Yasovarman (c. AD 925 to 950)

The Khajuraho stone inscription of AD 1002 states that Harsha's wife, Kanchuka, bore to him a son named Yasovarmandeva, who was pious and munificent, and who firmly established his rule by subduing other kings.[43] He is also mentioned as Lakshmanvarman in the same inscription.[44] With Yasovarman, the artistic scene attains more refinement and the town gains greater prosperity. Temples begin to be constructed on a lavish scale and in the ornate Nagara style of architecture. Yasovarman obtained the prestigious Vaikuntha Vishnu image from the Pratihara Devapala and built a magnificent temple, now called 'Lakshman', to specially install this precious image. We can imagine the glory of this temple which was a symbol of the Chandellas' victory over the Pratiharas and a record of the supremacy of their power. It was the first at Khajuraho to be built on such a grand scale and profusely adorned with sculptures.[45] The earlier temples, namely, the 'Brahma', and 'Lalguan Mahadeva' were very small and simple structures with much adornment. Yasovarman must have invited a gifted architect and his *silpi* to Khajuraho expressly to build this temple. Its splendid architecture reflects the affluence of the patron king and the augumented power of the Chandella dynasty. The numerous scenes of soldiers, cavalry and elephants in procession depicted on the platform reflect the might of the king who had subdued his overload.[46] The most significant achievement of Yasovarman was the conquest of Kalanjara. A Khajuraho inscription states, "He easily conquered the Kalanjara mountain, the dwelling place of Siva, which is so high that it impedes the progress of the Sun at mid-day."[47] The question as to whom Yasovarman conquered Kalanjara from is a controversial one.[48] Yasovarman also installed a huge image of the Varaha, who in Hindu mythology rescued the Prithvi from primeval waters, had become a political metaphor in India from the fifth century AD, and symbolised the king saving the earth by destroying enemies. By installing the mightly Varaha at Khajuraho, Yasovarman asserted his own power.[49] He certainly seems to have created a lasting impression on the popular mind, poetically described by Chandella court poet Madhava in the following words:

> In the halls of princes, where sages dwell (and) where good people meet, in the village, in the assemblages of lowly, among the rows of shops of merchants, (and) where streets cross, where wanderers talk together on the road (land) in the huts of the dwellers of the forest, everywhere, every body constantly from astonishment is loud only in praise of his excellencies.[50]

The inscription gives us a graphic picture of Chandella society and life of the different kinds of people. Similarly, Chandella sculptures depict every aspect of human life from birth to decay, every phase of our imagination, realistic or otherwise portrayed with great delicacy through the chisel of the artists of Chandellas. Thus, art activities started in full form during his reign. An inscription also credits him with the excavation of a big tank, which may be identical with one of the tanks situated in and around the village of Khajuraho.[51] Yasovarman was one of the most remarkable rulers of his times who patronised art activities.

7. Dhangadeva (c. AD 950-999)

Dhanga, the son and successor of Yasovarman born to his queen Puppa (Puspa) Devi,[52] was undoubtedly the most remarkable ruler of Chandella dynasty. He had consecrated the Lakshmana temple as his father died before it was completed. Dhanga was the first independent Chandella king who did not recognise the sovereignty of the Pratiharas. According to a Khajuraho inscriptions, he ruled over the earth, playfully acquired by the action of his long and strong arm, so far as Kalanjara and as far as Bhasvat, situated on the banks of Malava, from here also to the frontiers of the Chedi country and even as far as that mountain called Gopa.[53] This passage giving the precise limits of the dominion of the Chandella king is unique in the epigraphs. He was one of the leading powers of northern India, compared in might with 'Hamvira,' the contemporary Ghaznavid invader Subuktigin.

Dhanga's love and patronage of the arts has been specially mentioned in the inscription of AD 954, which praises him "as a source of munificence, bravery, discernment of arts and dalliance (kala-vilasa) of intelligence, majesty and might ...." It further states Dhanga's love for his people and his wish that they may obtain satisfaction.[54] The extant building at Khajuraho also bear witness to the remarkable art activities during the reign of Dhanga. An inscription informs us that he had erected there a magnificent temple in which two *linga*s were installed, one of emerald and the other of ordinary stone. This temple has been identified with the temple of Visvanatha. Undoubtedly, it is one of the most well preserved and lavishly ornamented temples at Khajuraho. The inscription has also immortalized the name of the architect, Chiccha, variously styled as Vijnanin, Visvakarma, Sutradhara and Dharmadhara.[55] Dhanga assumed the title of 'Sri Kalanjaradhipathi'.[56] He was a devotee of Siva. But he was not a narrow-minded sectarian. He extended his patronage to the Jain saint Pahila.[57] He was also a good administrator. He lived for more than a century and thought it fit to end his life at the confluence of the Ganga and Yamuna.[58] Dhanga not only expanded and consolidated his paternal kingdom, but also played a leading role in contemporary politics. His stable regime was conducive to the flourishing of the arts.

8. Gandadeva (c. AD 999 to 1002)

Gandadeva was the son and successor of Dhanga. He ruled for a few years according to the changed chronology of Chandella rulers on the basis of Kundeshwar copper-plate inscription of Queen Satyabhama, the wife of King Vidyadhara.[59] We have not even a single inscription of the ruler so far, but his name and achievements figure in the records of his successors.[60] Due to his short rule, we have little information regarding the art activities. As Dhangadeva lived a long life of about hundred years, in his old age it is Gandadeva who probably ruled as the crown prince. Prabhasa, the chief minister in Dhanga's time, continued in that office during the rule of Gandadeva.[61] Cunningham believed that the Visvanatha temple inscription placed after Dhanga's death was composed during the reign of Gandadeva.[62]

9. Vidyadhara (c. AD 1003-1035)

He was the son and successor of Gandadeva. King Vidyadhara was one of the most powerful Indian rulers of his time as described by Ibu-ul-Athir.[63] He played an important role in mobilising the Indian princes against the raids of Mahmud of Ghazni.[64] Particularly mentionable was the invasion of AD 1022, when Mahmud invaded the fort of Kalanjara, 'which has no equal in the whole country of Hindustan in impregnability'.[65] Under him the Chandella kingdom reached the zenith of its prosperity, and also won victories over the Kalachuris and the Paramaras, the two contemporary rivals in Central India. To celebrate his victory he built the grandest temple at Khajuraho, the Kandariya-Mahadeva.[66] Thus, he continued the temple building tradition of his predecessors. The Kandariya-Mahadeva temple is also the largest and grandest temple of Khajuraho. Vidyadhara's claims to greatness, however, does not rest so much on conquests and aggrandisements as on the gallant part played in organising resistance to the Ghaznavid invader. His reign marks the zenith of the Chandellas who emerged as the greatest power in northern India after the collapse of the Gurjara-Pratihara Empire. The sphere of his influence was much wider than the extent of his dominions.[67]

10. Vijayapala (c. AD 1035-1050)

Vidyadhara's son and successor was Vijayapala.[68] During Vijayapala's reign, the Chandellas probably also lost control which Vidyadhara exercised over the Kacchapaghatas of Gwalior.[69] Thus, in spite of the absence of any direct evidence, we have reason to believe that immediately after the death of Vidyadhara, there was a change in the fortunes of the Chandellas. The empire founded by Dhanga and expanded by Vidyadhara showed visible signs of decline during the time of Vijayapala.

11. Devavarman (c. AD 1050-1060)

Devavarman, the son of Vijayapala, has not been mentioned in the later records of the family, but his existence is well established by the Nanyaura and Charkhari copper-plates issued by him. His Nanyaura copper-plate dated VS 1107 (AD 1051) mentioned him as the son of Vijayapala and grandson of Vidyadharadeva.[70] The inscription names the mother of Devavarmandeva as Bhuvanadevi.[71] In later Chandella inscriptions, the name of Devavarmandeva is omitted from the family genealogy. These inscriptions mention Kirtivarman as the son and successor of Vijayapala.[72] He was defeated by the Kalachuri king, Lakshmikarna.[73] Therefore, the reign period of Devavarman particularly may be regarded to have proved to be a dark period for the Chandellas. It was most probably due to this that the Chandellas did not like to recount the condition during this period in the records of the later rulers.[74] He uses the title of 'Kalanjaradhipati,' which shows that though the Chandellas ruler might have suffered defeat at the hands of Kalachuri king Lakshmikarna, yet he retained his hold on the strategic fortress of Kalanjara.[75] His great regard for his mother, Bhuvanadevi, is evident from the Nanyaura copper-plate, which was issued by him on the occasion of the death anniversary.[76]

12. Kirtivarman (c. AD 1060-1100)

He was the son of Vijayapala and grandson of Vidyadhara. The Chandellas re-emerged as an important political power in Central India. There is epigraphical as well as literary evidence for his victory over the Kalachuri king, Lakshmikarna. The Ajaigarh inscription compares Kirtivarman with the pitcher born Agastya who swallowed Karna, the ocean,[77] and the Mahoba inscription likens him to Vishnu Purushottama who churned the ocean and won Lakshmi together with the elephants.[78] Again, Kirtivarman is compared with Purushottama in the play *Prabodha Chandrodaya* of Krishna Misra staged before Kirtivarman at the command of his general Gopala who had vanquished Kalachuri king Karna and placed Kirtivarman on the throne.[79] It is also significant to note that the first Chandella coins were issued in the reign of

King Kirtivarman. He built temples at Ajaigarh, Kalanjara, and Mahoba.[80] He also built lakes at Mahoba, Chanderi and Kalanjara. There is a fort in his name, Kirtidurga, on the Betwa River, constructed by his minister Vatsraja.[81]

13. Jayavarman (c. AD 1110-1120)

The next ruler after Kirtivarman is his grandson, Jayavarman who was devoted to the worship of Narayana. The Chaturbhuja temple of Khajuraho with the sublime image of the ascetic god (Narayana) with 'Jata' assignable to about AD 1100, was possibly constructed by Jayavarman. In AD 1117 Jayavarman had the Visvanatha temple inscription rewritten as the original record of AD 999 had become illegible. This indicates that even 120 years after its construction, the Visvanatha temple was well managed and that it was then known as Marakateshwara after the emerald *linga,* which must have still been *in situ*. According to an inscription of Kalanjara,[82] Jayavarman voluntarily abdicated the throne, wearied as he was of the government, and "proceeded to the divine river to wash away his sins".[83]

14. Mandanavarman (c. AD 1128-1165)

He was the son and successor of Prithvivarman. During the reign of Madanavarman, a large number of inscriptions and coins were found from various Chandella towns indicating widespread trade and prosperity. Several lakes and temples were built by the king in different parts of Jejakabhukti. Those at Mahoba and Madana Sagarapura (Tikamgarh district), though now in ruined condition, preserve his memory. The Gujarat chronicles describe the magnificence of his court and the economic prosperity of his kingdom.[84] At Khajuraho, the last great temple locally known as the Duladeva can be assigned to Madanavarman.[85] This temple displays a marked change in its sculptural style from the earliest temples in that its figures have sharp features and angular postures, and wear typical trefoil crowns and *padaugada* as ornaments.[86] An inscription from Kalanjara refers to the chief dancer, Padmavati, during his reign at Kalanjara.[87] Madanavarman was a great patron of art and culture.

15. Parmaradideva (c. AD 1165-1203)

He was the grandson of Madanavarman, who was a patron of artists, poets and scholars.[88] His rivalry with King Prithviraja Chamana has been recorded in the *Prithviraja Raso* and the *Parmala Raso*.[89]

He himself composed an inscription in praise of Siva at Kalanjara.[90] He was defeated by Qutubuddin Aibak in 1202 following which the power of the Chandellas began to decline. Parmaradideva is known for the patronage of art and promotion of learning.[91] A number of monuments in different parts of Bundelkhand are associated with him, particularly at Kalanjara and Ajaigarh.[92]

16. Trailokyavarman (c. AD 1203-1245)

He was the next powerful ruler. The Ajaigarh rock inscription of Kalyandevi states that "Trailokyavarman" ruled the kingdom after Parmaradideva.[93] The most important achievement of Trailokyavarman was the reconquest of Kalanjara, which had been captured by Qutubuddin Aibak.[94] Trailokyavarman had a fairly long reign and during his time he also patronised artistic activities, particularly at Kalanjara and Ajaigarh.[95] Trailokyavarman had given a land grant to one Ranta, whose father was killed in the battlefield without any condition by way of maintenance for death (*mritukavritti*).[96] This indicates that sacrifice of life was honoured by the Chandella kings.

17. Viravarman (c. AD 1250-1286)

He was the successor of Trailokyavarman. The Ajaigarh stone inscription of Ganapati states that he had installed the image of Dani Vinayaka at Ajaigarh fort.[97] Another inscription from the same place records the construction of a *Nirjara-kupa* at Ajaigarh and tank and hall at Nandipura by Viravarman's queen, Kalyanadevi.[98] The Kalanjara inscription refers to Viravarman's work of public utility. He is credited with the construction of various temples, gardens, ponds and tanks, and with the installation of the images of Siva, Kamala and Kali.[99] Similarly, an Ajaigarh inscription refers to the installation of a Jain image during his reign.[100]

18. Bhojavarman (c. AD 1286-1288)

He was the last important ruler of Chandella dynasty. An Ajaigarh rock inscription refers to the construction of a temple by Subhata at that place. The temple must have been dedicated to Siva.[101]

The Chandella kings not only constructed temples and tanks, but also encouraged literature, dance, music and other fine arts. The refined culture of Chandella period is reflected in the visual art of the Chandellas. Thus, the political condition of the Chandella period had a significant role in the study of Chandella monuments and their chronology.

NOTES AND REFERENCES

1. Febvre Lucien, *A Geographical Introduction to History*, p. 9.
2. M.L. Nigam, *Cultural History of Bundelkhand*, p. 3.
3. *Ibid.*, p. 5.
4. *Imperial Gazetteer of India*, Vol. VIII, p. 16.
5. S.K. Mitra, *Early Rulers of Khajuraho*, p. 5.
6. M.L. Nigam, *op. cit.*, p. 4.
7. *Ibid.*, p. 5.
8. *Ibid.*
9. N.S. Bose, *History of the Chandellas*, p. 134.
10. *Ibid.*
11. *Ibid.*, p. 172.
12. *Ibid.*
13. *Ibid.*, p. 173.
14. R.K. Dikshit, *Chandellas of Jejakabhukti*, Preface, p. vi.
15. *Parmal Raso*, pp. 9-11.
16. Devangana Desai, *The Religious Imagery of Khajuraho*, p. 39.
17. Devangana Desai, *Khajuraho*.
18. *Epigraphia Indica*, Vol. I, p. 123, V. 10.
19. *Ibid.*, p. 141.
20. *Ibid.*, pp. 125, 131.
21. *Ibid.*
22. *Ibid.*, Vol. I, p. 141.
23. *Ibid.*
24. *Ibid.*, pp. 125, 131.
25. *Ibid.*, pp. 125-26, 131, V. 13.
26. *Ibid.*, pp. 125, 131.
27. *Ibid.*, p. 126, V. 14-15.
28. *Ibid.*, p. 221, V. 10, p. 122, L. 6.
29. *Ibid.*, p. 141, V. 18.
30. *Ibid.*, p. 221.

31. H.C. Ray, *Dynastic History of Northern India*, Vol. II, p. 671.
32. *Epigraphia Indica*, Vol. I, pp. 126, 131.
33. *Ibid.*, p. 142.
34. *Indian Antiquary*, Vol. XV, p. 283.
35. *A.S.I.R.*, Vol. VII, p. 41.
36. *J.A.S.B.* (1881), p. 8.
37. *Indian Antiquary*, Vol. XVII, p. 202, L. 1.
38. *Epigraphia Indica*, Vol. I, p. 126.
39. *Ibid.*, Vol. II, p. 306, V. 8.
40. *Ibid.*, Vol. I, p. 122.
41. Devangana Desai, *The Religious Imagery of Khajuraho*, p. 41.
42. *Ibid.*, fn. 26.
43. *Epigraphia Indica*, Vol. 1, p. 126, V. 23.
44. *Ibid.*, p. 128, V. 17.
45. Devangana Desai, *The Religious Imagery of Khajuraho*, p. 41.
46. *Ibid.*
47. *Epigraphia Indica*, Vol. 1, pp. 127-28, V. 31.
48. N.S. Bose, *op. cit.*, p. 56.
49. Devangana Desai, *Khajuraho*, p. 10.
50. *Epigraphia Indica*, Vol. I, pp. 128-29, 134.
51. *Ibid.*, pp. 129, 134, V. 43.
52. *Ibid.*, p. 144.
53. *Ibid.*, p. 129.
54. Devangana Desai, *The Religious Imagery of Khajuraho*, p. 42.
55. *Ibid.*
56. *Indian Antiquary*, Vol. XVI, p. 203.
57. Devangana Desai, *The Religious Imagery of Khajuraho*, p. 42.
58. *Epigraphia Indica*, Vol. I, p. 146, V. 55.
59. S.K. Sullerey, 'Fresh light on chronology of Chandella', *The Journal of Asiatic Society of Bombay*, Vol. 73 (New Series), pp. 190-94.
60. R.K. Dikshit, *op. cit.*, p. 70.
61. *Epigraphia Indica*, Vol. 1, pp. 197, 204.
62. Devangana Desai, *The Religious Imagery of Khajuraho*, p. 42.
63. R.K. Dikshit, *op. cit.*, p. 89, fn. 1.
64. Devangana Desai, *Khajuraho*, p. 10.
65. S.K. Mitra, *op. cit.*, p. 81.
66. Krishna Deva, *Khajuraho*, p. 5
67. R.K. Dikshit, *op. cit.*, p. 78.
68. *Epigraphia Indica*, Vol. 1, pp. 197-98, 203.
69. N.S. Bose, *op. cit.*, p. 69.
70. *Indian Antiquary*, Vol. XVI, p. 206.
71. S.K. Mitra, *op. cit.*, p. 93.
72. *Ibid.*, p. 91.
73. *Ibid.*, p. 92.
74. *Ibid.*
75. *Ibid.*
76. *Ibid.*, p. 93.
77. *Epigraphia Indica*, Vol. 1, p. 327.
78. *Ibid.*, p. 219.
79. Devangana Desai, *The Religious Imagery of Khajuraho*, p. 45.
80. *Ibid.*
81. *Ibid.*

82. *A.S.I.R.*, Vol. XXI, p. 39.
83. Devangana Desai, *The Religious Imagery of Khajuraho*, p. 45.
84. *Ibid.*
85. *Ibid.*
86. *Ibid.*
87. *A.S.I.R.*, Vol. XXI, p. 34.
88. R.K. Dikshit, *op. cit.*, pp. 150-51.
89. *Ibid.*
90. *J.A.S.B.*, Vol. XVII, 1848, pp. 313-18.
91. R.K. Dikshit, *op. cit.*, p. 151.
92. *A.S.I.R.*, Vol. XXI, pp. 46-47.
93. *Epigraphia Indica*, Vol. XVI, pp. 272-77.
94. R.K. Dikshit, *op. cit.*, p. 157.
95. S.K. Sullerey, *Ajaigarh Aur Kalanjara ki Devapratimayain*, p. 75.
96. *Epigraphia Indica*, Vol. XVI, pp. 275-76.
97. *A.S.I.R.*, Vol. XXI, p. 52.
98. *Epigraphia Indica*, Vol. I, pp. 325-30.
99. *A.S.I.R.*, Vol. XXI, pp. 38-40.
100. R.K. Dikshit, *op. cit.*, Appendix A, pp. 207-08.
101. *Epigraphia Indica*, Vol. I, pp. 325-330.

2

Main Centres of Chandella Art and Architecture and Their Natural Surroundings

The Chandellas of Jejakabhukti occupied a prominent position among the ruling dynasties of early medieval India. They played a very significant role in the political and cultural life of early medieval history of India. They ruled over Jejakabhukti region for about six centuries, which is rather unusual in the history of the ruling dynasties in India.[1] The Chandella kings were great builders and patrons of art and letters. Jejakabhukti was blessed with prosperity and political stability and swept between tenth and twelfth centuries by a cultural upheaval manifesting itself in much charm and vigour. The Chandella court was adorned by poets like Madhava, Rama, Nandana, Gadadhara and Jagnaik and the dramatist Krishna Misra, author of *Prabodha Chandrodaya* and *Vatsaraja*. The Chandellas decorated their kingdom with temples, palaces, forts, lakes and tanks, which were mainly centred in their strongholds of Kalanjara, Ajaigarh (Jayapura durga)[2] and Mahoba (Mahotsava-nagara), and in lesser degrees to their towns of Dudhai, Chandpur, Madanpur and Deogarh. But none of these places could be compared in magnificence with Khajuraho, which was adorned by the Chandellas with tanks and temples. According to the local tradition, the place had originally eighty-five temples,[3] but only twenty-five now remain in different stages of preservation.

Before studying the main centres of Chandella art and architecture, we must know the region over which the monuments were constructed during the Chandella period. The frontiers of the Chandella kingdom varied from time to time but the area roughly corresponded to what is now known as Bundelkhand. At the zenith of Chandella power in the eleventh century, this region was bounded on all four sides by rivers – in the north by Yamuna, in the south by Narmada, in the east by the Tamasa, and in the west by the Chambal.[4] The track was known during the sixth century BC as Chedi,[5] during Chandella times as Jejakabhukti,[6] and since the fourteenth century as Bundelkhand.[7] In ancient times, the region played a glorious role in the political and cultural history of India. According to local tradition, the *asramas* of such famous *rishis* as Valmiki, Vedavyasa, Atri and Agastya were located here.[8] The region is also famous for its numerous lakes, formed by erecting embankments across the streams. The province is rich in natural resources, and is traversed by many branches of the Vindhyas and still more numerous rivers, rivulets and forest; it is remarkable for its natural surroundings and beauty, which even attracted the notice of Rama.[9] Thus, geographical features influence the physical and mental activities of a concerned area. The mountains, rivers, forests, fauna-flora, animals, reptiles and birds are reflected in art. Similarly, the racial features of the people are also reflected in the Chandellas art and architecture. The numerous art motifs and decorative pattern and designs are taken from the natural surroundings of the region. The rocks of the region provided artists the material for construction of temples, caves, tanks, ponds and sculptures. Similarly, the stone quarries of Panna provided sandstone for the construction of temples and sculptures at Khajuraho. A panel kept in the Khajuraho museum depicts a large number of labourers for carrying stones with the help of long wooden pole.[10] The diamond mines at Panna and adjoining region are equally added to the ruler's richness to construct high profile temples at Khajuraho and other art centres. The geographical factor plays a very significant role in the study of art and architecture of any region. The same is the case with Chandella art.

In the sphere of art and architecture, the region played a significant role. So far as art tradition is concerned, art activities started in this area as early as the pre-historic period. Many pre-historic rock painting sites have been discovered in the Jejakabhukti region.[11] Sculptural art activities began in this region during the reign of Sungas from c. 200 BC with Bharhut.[12] *Jataka* stories emerged for the first time in the carving of Bharhut.[13] This is a significant contribution of Bharhut to Indian art. Again, during the Gupta times, the main centres evolved at Bhumara, Koha, Nachna, Eran, Vidisha and Deogarh. The Parvati temple at Nachna,[14] the Siva temple at Bhumara, Visnu temple at Eran, rock-cut caves at Udaigiri, and Dasavatara temple at Deogarh form a significant stage in the development of Gupta temple architecture. Depiction of scenes from the *Ramayana* started in Indian art from Nachna.[15] Similarly, the sculptures of Ganga and Yamuna also came into existence during this period from this region. In the seventh century AD Chaturmukha temple at Nachna, one of the earliest typical Sikhara temples of north India[16] is more important and constitutes a significant phase in architecture, marking the termination between the Gupta and medieval temples styles.[17] The building tradition was continued by the Pratiharas who left in the region their finest temple, one at Barwasagar – the Jarai-Matha – and two other Sun temples at Mankhera and Umri (Tikamgarh Distt.) assigned to circa ninth century AD.[18] Under the supremacy of the Pratiharas, simpler shrines of provincial style made of granite were also erected in this region at sites like Manu-Suhaniya,[18] Kinari and Chamaru, all located in Chhatarpur district.[20] This was the art and architectural background of Jejakabhukti region before the rise of the Chandellas. It also gives us an idea of the origin and development of art tradition in the region.

These four places – Khajuraho, Kalanjara, Mahoba and Ajaigarh – comprised the vital centre of Chandella kingdom.[21] Smith's conjecture that Khajuraho was the religious and Mahoba the civil capital of Chandellas may not be altogether wide off the mark. Kalanjara, of course, since the conquest by Yasovarman, remained their most important military base. Ajaigarh was another important military centre.[22] The irregular quadrilateral form by these places was the centre of Chandella power.[23] These four places comprised the main art centres of Chandella kingdom.[24] The Ken River runs through the country from south to north dividing it into two nearby equal portions, with the capital cities of Mahoba and Khajuraho in the western half and the great forts of Kalanjara and Ajaigarh in the eastern half.[25] The position of the Chandellas was strengthened by the possession of the important and almost inaccessible forts of Ajaigarh, Mahoba and Kalanjara. The importance of these three forts to the Chandella kingdom is clearly evident from the history of the dynasty.[26] The Chandella forts were not only military and religious centres but also art centres, which have not been studied by scholars so far. A review[27] of the works so far published on Chandella art and architecture reveals that mostly studies on Chandella art and architecture are focused around Khajuraho. Scholars are so overwhelmed with the magnificence of Khajuraho that they overlook the other centres of Chandella art and architecture.[28] An attempt has been made to study the Chandella forts of Kalanjara, Ajaigarh[29] and Mahoba as art centres of Chandella art and architecture. A detailed study of the art and architecture of Kalanjara, Ajaigarh, Mahoba and Khajuraho is included in the present chapter.

KALANJARA

The fort of Kalanjara, in the Banda district of Uttar Pradesh, stands as a sentinel guarding the pathway of central India. It is the strongest fort in north India and the most significant stronghold of Chandella area. Kalanjara, though famous as a religious and military centre of India, was also an important art centre of its time.

The famous fort of Kalanjara was occupied as a place of considerable significance in the cultural and political history of India. Kalanjara fort (Latitude 25° 1′ N and Longitude 80° 29′ E), situated on a lofty crag of precious rock of hard sandstone on an outlying branch of the Panna range, is at a distance of about 57 km to the south-east of Banda and 87 km from Satna (M.P.). Kalanjara fort has an elevation of 375 metres from the sea level and about 215 metres from the surrounding plains.[30] The total area of Kalanjara fort is about 2850 hectares.[31] The town of Kalanjara is located at the foot of the hill. It contains many antiquities, remains of ramparts and three gates, which are the significant features of town planning. The location of these gates are sufficiently indicated by their names, the Kamata (Chitrakuta) Gate lying to the north, the Panna Gate to the south-west, and Rewa Gate to the south-east of the town.

Situated in the midst of Vindhyan forest (Vindhyatavi), Kalanjara attracted the attention of ancient sages, who found the site very congenial for penances. Literary accounts indicate that several saints had their *asramas* in and around the present site of Kalanjara.[32] Kalanjara has been occupied from the most remote times. According to Wilson, it is mentioned in the Vedas as one of the *tapasya-sthanas* or "spots adopted to practices of austere devotion".[33] This indicates the sanctity of the hill of Kalanjara as a resort of *tapaswis* or holy ascetics. The overhanging rocks afforded shelter to the *Rishis*, and the rainwater percolating through the rocks from above gave them water to drink. The hills of Asirgarh and Gwalior were similarly occupied by holy ascetics before they were made into fortresses. At the former, the famous saint Aswathama gave his name to Aswathamagiri, and at the latter place the holy hermit Gwalipa gave his name to Gwali-awar.[34] But the name of Kalanjaradri, or the hill of Kalanjara, is said to have been derived from Siva himself, who, as *kāla*, or 'Time', causes all things to decay (*jara*), and who is therefore the destroyer of all things and the god of death. *Tapaswis*, or ascetics, of Kalanjara were therefore devoted to the worship of Siva.[35]

According to Wilson, Kalanjara is mentioned in the Vedas and it was one of *tapasya-sthanas* or "spots adopted for practices of austere devotion". By a very slight change the Greek Tamasis may be read as 'tapasis'.[36] The identification of Wilson and Cunningham seems reasonable. Thus, Kalanjara was more than a fort and a military centre; it has been a sacred *tirtha* also. In *Satayuga,* it was known as Ratankuta, while in the *Tretayuga* and *Dvaparayuga* it was known as Mahagiri and Pingala.[37] The glorification of Kalanjara as a *tirtha* is referred to in the *Mahabharata*. It is stated that whoever bathes in the lake of the gods in Kalanjara, acquires the same merit as if he had made a gift of one thousand cows. It was also considered a very famous mountain during this period.[38] In the same epic it is also described that 'Hiranyavindu' is located at Kalanjara.[39] Similarly, it is also mentioned that if one takes bath at Kalanjara for one month, he acquires the merit of horse-sacrifice.[40] During the epic period, Kalanjara developed as a *tirthasthal*. In the *Valmiki Ramayana,* it is mentioned that Rama appointed a Brahman the *Kulapati* of Kalanjara. This episode indicates that at this time Kalanjara was a well established centre of Saivism.[41] This fact is also corroborated from the seals of Bhita discovered from the excavations.[42] Some of the religious seals bear different appellations of Siva, such as 'Kalesvara', Kalanjara-bhattarka, Bhadresvara, Mahesvara and Nandini – the last being the name of his mount; one of the oval seals in Marshall's list[43] has a trident-axe flanked by a diagram of dots, really a hill symbol and unidentified emblem on its left, the legend in eastern Gupta characters is *Kalesvara priyatama* (may Kalesvara be pleased). Marshall observes that Kalesvara is the name of a *Sivalinga,* according to *Skanda Purana,* and this tablet would seem to have been presented as an offering to some shrine of Bhita.[44] The seal next in the list is also Saiva in nature; it bears a realistic *Sivalinga* with an umbrella on one side and a trident on the other. The *linga* is placed on a hill in the form of a well arranged pile of round balls, below which is a wave probably standing for a river; the legend in northern Gupta characters is *Kalanjara bhattarakasya,* i.e., 'of the lord of Kalanjara'. This seal was evidently issued from a Saiva shrine on the Kalanjara hill.[45] Another seal from Bhita having a legend *Kalanjara* in northern Gupta characters belongs to Kalanjara.[46] One more seal bearing the legend in north Gupta characters is *'Bhadresvara'*. Marshall says that this is the name of the *Sivalinga* of Kalpagamma according to *Vamana Purana.*[47] But, in one rock inscription from Kalanjara, we find reference to a brick temple of Bhadresvara constructed at Kalanjara during the time of Panduvamsi Udayan. On the basis of this inscription, now we can identify the Bhadresvara of Bhita seal with Bhadresvara of Kalanjara.[48] These seals indicate the prevalence of Saivism in Kalanjara. Thus, during the epic period, Kalanjara became a famous *tirtha* and centre of *Saivism*.

There is a good amount of Puranic literature which throws light on the different aspects of religious life at Kalanjara.[49] In the *Padma Purana,* it is named as one of the nine 'Ukhalas' (holy places) in northern India.[50] In the same *Purana,* it is mentioned that Kalanjara is able to destroy and burn great sins.[51] Similarly, *Brahma Purana* also mentions it to be a destroyer of all sins.[52] In the *Garuda Purana,* Kalanjara is described as giver of salvation.[53] The *Padama* and *Skanda Purana*s mention it respectively as 'Brahmakshetra'[54] and 'Purshottamakshetra'.[55] Kalanjara is also known as 'Ravikshetra'.[56]

During the Puranic period, Kalanjara was considered as one of the great *tirthas* of northern India. In the *Garuda Purana* it is designated as 'Maha tirtha',[57] in the *Padma Purana* as 'Uttama tritha',[58] in the *Agni*[59] and *Brahma Puranas*[60] as 'Parama tirtha,' and in the *Matsya Purana* as an auspicious and superior pilgrimage centre.[61]

Kalanjara is also related to 'Pitrapuja' and it is mentioned in *Vayu Purana*[62] and *Brahamanda Puranas*[63] as a place of 'Sradha-Dana'.

The Puranic literature throws good light on the relationship of Kalanjara with Siva. In *Vayu,*[64] *Linga*[65] and *Kurma*[66] *Purana*s, it is stated that Siva destroyed the 'Kala' in this place, and that is why it is called Kalanjara. In the *Purana*s, Kalanjara is mentioned as an abode, Nilakantha. In the *Vamana Purana,* Nilakantha is mentioned as Kalanjara.[67] Kalanjara is also referred to as the abode of Nilakantha in the Khajuraho inscription of Dhanga Chandella.[68] Similarly, an inscription of Chandella king, Kirtivarman from Ajaigarh also described the worship of Nilakantha.[69] An inscription from Kalanjara, during the time of Madanavarman refers to the worship of Nilakantha by Maha Pratihara Sangrama Simha and Maha Nachani Padmavati.[70] Both were attached to this temple. The temple of Nilakantha was the main attraction of pilgrims.[71]

The Puranic literature also described Kalanjara as a *Saktipitha*. In the *Padma*,[72] *Matsya*[73] and *Devi-Bhagavata Puranas*,[74] Kalanjara is mentioned as the abode of Kali.

The Puranic myth is connected with the different births of seven *rishis*, which is also connected with Kalanjara referred to in the *Harivamsa*,[75] *Agni*[76] and *Padma*[77] *Puranas*. This Puranic episode is related with Mrigadhara at Kalanjara, which is connected with the Sradha Dana. This episode is referred to in Jain[78] and Buddhist literature.[79]

There is a good amount of folk literature which throws welcome light on Kalanjara's significance as a great religious centre. The epigraphs of pilgrimage found at Kalanjara also state that it was a very popular religious centre.[80]

When Kalanjara transformed as a fort is a matter of controversy. According to Cunningham, it seems highly probable that the fortress of Kalanjara may have been founded at least as early as the beginning of the Christian Era.[81] Firishta suggests that it was built by the king Kedar in seventh century AD.[82] But we have no reference of this ruler in any other source. While traditional stories give the credit for construction of this fort to Chandravarman,[83] these stories are not supported by epigraphic sources. The Khajuraho inscription of Dhanga informs us that the Chandella ruler Yasovarman occupied this fort for the first time.[84] This was considered a great achievement by Yasovarman, which enhanced the prestige of the family and the Chandellas came to be recoginsed as a political power. Of the eight forts ascribed to the Chandellas by tradition, Kalanjara is most important and it is believed to have been the military centre of this kingdom.[85] The sturdy defences of Kalanjara provided them a comparative security against external and internal enemies. The whole history of the Chandellas has centred round the historic fort of Kalanjara and, to a lesser degree, the fort of Ajaigarh.[86] It was also signified by the assumption of the epithet "Kalanjaradhipati" by the Chandella ruler from the time of Dhanga Chandella.[87] The Khajuraho inscription of Dhanga states, "He playfully acquired by the action of his long arms, as far as Kalanjara, and as far as Bhasvat situated on the banks of the river of Malva; from here also to the banks of the river Kalindi, and from here also to the frontier of Chedi country, and even as far as that mountain called Gopa."[88] The Chandella Vidyadhara was the most powerful ruler of the Chandella dynasty. He had the distinction of being the only Indian ruler who effectively checked the triumphal career of Sultan Mahmud and saved his kingdom from destruction by the ruthless conqueror.[89] The sturdy fort of Kalanjara played a vital role in protecting the Chandella kingdom and the temples of Khajuraho.[90] According to Muslim writers, the fort of Kalanjara has no equal in the whole of the country of Hindustan for strength and impregnability.[91] It is mentioned in one inscription to be as strong as the 'Wall of Alexandar'.[92] In the Khajuraho inscription of AD 998, Dhanga is given the epithet 'Kalanjaradhipati', the first use of this title by a Chandella king.[93]

From the post-Gupta period to the late medieval period, Kalanjara developed as religious, political and art centre of significance. During the rule of the dynasties of the Panduvamsi,[94] the Kalachuris,[95] the Gurjara-Pratiharas,[96] and the Chandellas,[97] several rulers of these dynasties took pride in the sanctity of the Kalanjara. They contributed largely to the enrichment and preservation of religious traditions and development of art and culture at Kalanjara. During the rule of the Chandellas, Kalanjara developed as a power centre and also as a centre of art and cultural activities. During this period Kalanjara reached its zenith.

The antiquities of Kalanjara were first noticed by Pogson,[98] but they have been since described in detail by Maisey[99] in an interesting paper accompanied by numerous illustrations. Cunningham made a significant contribution in his Report, Vol. XXI, to study the antiquities of Kalanjara afresh and he discovered many inscriptions of historical and cultural significance at Kalanjara.[100] He also prepared a map of the fort site. He for the first time wrote the history of the

Chandella dynasty on the basis of material available to him. Thus, Cunningham's contribution is very significant in the study of Chandella history and antiquities.[101]

There are two entrances to the fort of Kalanjara, of which the main is on the north side towards the town, and the other at the south-east angle towards Panna, which is still called the Panna Gate (now closed). Now, a road has been constructed by the Uttar Pradesh Government, which has made it easy to reach the fort. The north entrance has seven different gates which are named as following:

1. Alam, or Alamgiri, Gate
2. Ganes Gate
3. Chandi, or Chan-burji Gate
4. Buddha-bhadra Gate
5. Hanuman Gate
6. Lal Darwaza and
7. Bara Darwaza

The number of seven gates suggested to Pogson that Kalanjara must have been the "seat of solar 'worship' which is supposed to be confirmed by the name of Ravi Chitra".[102] But it is not Ravi Chitra, it is 'Ravikshetra'. Though the Kalanjara is associated with Sun worship, this theory is not acceptable because previously there were only six gates, the lowest gate named Alam Darwaza having been added during the reign of Aurangzeb.[103]

There is an ascent of about 200 feet up to the lowest gate, which is a battlement building in the modern Mughal style. Over the archway outside, there is a Persian inscription of three lines, inscribing the constructing of the gate by Muhammed Murad, during the reign of Emperor Aurangzeb, when it was made as strong as the 'Wall of Alexander'. This gate was constructed in AD 1673. Above the first gate there is a steep ascent, chiefly by steps, to the second gate named as Ganes Darwaza. At a short distance, higher up in the bend of the road, the third gate is found, named as Chandi Darwaza. As mentioned by Maisey, there is in fact a double gate with four towers, on which account it is also known as the Chauburji Darwaza, 'Gate of the four towers'. At this gateway there are several pilgrim's records of various dates. On the rock close by there is an inscription of fifteen lines, of the later Gupta period which has been discovered by Cunningham.[104] This inscription belongs to Panduvamsi Udayan and gives information of the brick temple of Bhadresvara constructed at Kalanjara.[105]

The fourth gate, named Buddha-bhadra Darwaza, is the gate of the 'auspicious planet Mercury Buddha'. It is also named the Swarga-rohana or 'heaven-ascending gate', owing to the stiff climb required to reach it. Near this there is a rock-cut pond and a Bhairava image.[106]

The fifth gate, Hanuman Darwaza, is named after a figure of the monkey-god carved on a slab resting against the rock. There is also a reservoir called Hanuman-kund. There are, besides, numerous rock-sculptures, which are very much weather-worn. Many, however, are still quite recognisable such as Siva and Parvati, Ganesa, the Nandi and the *linga*. On the ascent beyond there are many weather-worn figures carved on the rock representing Kali, Chandika and the *linga*. There is also a small cave containing a broken figure of Hanuman. There are several short inscriptions of pilgrims with dates.[106]

The sixth gate, called the Lal Darwaza, from its red colour, stands near the top of the ascent. To the west of this gate, in the *Raoni*, or faussebraie, immediately above the Bhairava-kund, there is a colossal figure of Bhairava cut in the rock. Here also are two figures of pilgrims represented carrying water in the usual manner in two vessels fixed to the end of a Banghi pole. Near one of them, there is the following inscription in well-shaped Gupta characters:

Samadhigata pannch-mahasobada Samanta Sri Vasanta.

"The illustrious Samanta Vasanta (the possessor of the title of panccha-mahasobdha)".[107] This title is commonly applied to Samanta or the petty chief. According to Cunningham, the figure of the water-carrier represents the Samant himself.[108] There is a long inscription much too obliterated to be readable. In the fourth line Cunningham read the name of Kalanjaradri or the 'Hill of Kalanjara'.[109]

A short ascent leads to the seventh, or uppermost, gate called 'Bara Darwaza' or the 'Main Gate'. As it stands now, it is undoubtedly modern, and late date is confirmed by the only inscription attached to it of Samvat 1691, or AD 1634.[110]

There are five rock-cut caves in the fort of Kalanjara. The rock-cut caves are situated not in a particular area, but they are located in different parts of the fort. Near the Bara-Darwaza is located a rock-cut cave called 'Sita Sej'. The cave has one stone bed and one stone pillow. This cave is associated with Sita, the wife of Rama. Close to 'Sita Sej' is Sita-kund, a natural reservoir. It is a pool of water in a small cavity under shelving rocks and is reached by two or three steps.

At a short distance from 'Sita Sej' on the eastern part of the hill there are two rock-cut caves known as 'Siddha ki Gupha' and 'Bhagwan ki Sej'. 'Siddha ki Gupha' is a small excavation in a perpendicular rock for performing penance. 'Bhagwan ki Sej' is a rock-cut cave under a projection of a rock. The cave has one bed and one stone pillow. There is a small cistern, now named 'Pani-ki-aman', with a small mouth. The roof of the cistern is supported by four decorated small pillars.

The biggest and the most significant of the entire rock-cut example is the cave of Nilakantha temple situated on the western slope of the fort. The upper gate, leading into the outwork, is attributed to the Chandella king Parmal, or Paramardideva. There are several inscriptions of a later period. A second gate, which leads into the courtyard of the temple, has no inscription. But on the rock on the right hand of the descent there are numerous small caves and niches, with several images and inscriptions. The rock-cut images are very important for the study of Chandella art. The Nilakantha temple consists of a rock-cut sanctum and structural *mandapa,* which was added during the time of the Chandella ruler Kirtivarman.[111] The interior of the sanctum is not square but oblong on plan. It contains a black stone *linga,* about 1.35 meters high known as Nilakantha Mahadeva. It is said that Siva came here after swallowing the poison which came out of the churning of the ocean, then digested the poison in his neck, the reason why he is called Nilakantha. The installed *linga* is also said to have originated itself and not installed by anyone. It is named as 'Svayambhuva Sivalinga'. The 'Svayambhuva linga' is said to have belonged to the 'Uttamottama' variety of *linga*s. The 'Svayambhuva linga' is described in the *Kamarkagama* as one which rose up and came into existence by itself and existed from times immemorial. Even if these are slightly damaged, they need no renovation (*Jirnodhara*). If, however, a 'Svayambhuva linga' is, for some reason or the other, completely removed from its setting and thrown out, the event would cause the king his destruction as also that of his kingdom since he and his officers are responsible for the safety of such a *linga*. In fact, a 'Svayambhuva linga' is considered so scared that it is above all the rules laid down in the *Agamas* for the other class of *linga*s. Sixty-nine places, situated in various parts of India, are said to possess 'Svayambhuva lingas', and a list of these places is given by Nigamayanadeva of Vyaghrapura, son of Vamadeva Sivacharya.[112] In this list we find the name of Nilakantha at Kalanjara.[113] We also find the mention of Nilakantha at Kalanjara in *Vaman Purana*.[114] In Dhanga's inscription of Khajuraho, Kalanjara is said to be the abode of Lord Nilakantha.[115] From one of the inscriptions of Kalanjara, we know that Mahapratihara Sangram Singh and Mahanachani Padmavati were attached to this temple and the deity.[116]

The appointment of Mahapratihara shows that he was in-charge of the security of the famous temple and Padmavati was in-charge of the royal dancers. The Chandella ruler, Paramardideva himself composed an euology of Lord Nilakantha.[117] It is at present the main object of worship and to judge by the pilgrim records, it has been equally popular for many centuries.[118] The façade of the cave is very rich in sculptures. On the jambs of the door there are also sculptures of Siva and Parvati with Ganga and Yamuna Rivers. These are of the Gupta period. The pillars of the hall are of later date and belong to the time of King Kirtivarman Chandella.[119] The roof of the pillars still remains, forming a square with four on each side, and four in the middle. In roofing the corners were cut off to form an octagon.

Just outside the *mandapa* of Nilakantha, there is a deep *kund*, or rock-cut reservoir, called 'Swarga-rohana'; and to the right of the *kund* in rock recess or niche, there is a colossal image of Kala Bhairva, 24 feet in height, standing on two feet of water. The sculpture is 17 feet broad. It is mentioned by Abdul Fazl as being 18 cubits in height.[120] The image has eighteen arms, and is ornamented with the usual garland of skulls, with snake amulets, and snakes twined round the neck. In the hands are various objects, of which the most prominent are a sword, a bowl of blood, etc. Beside this statue there is a figure of the skeleton Goddess Kali, 4 feet in height, which is now standing a foot deep in water .

There are more than a dozen structural temples in the fort of Kalanjara. All these temples are located around the tanks and reservoirs in different parts of the fort. These temples have been raised to the ground. To the east of the Nilakantha temple, there are ruins of several temples and an image of the Varaha in a good state of preservation. This image is fashioned on a fine-grained bluish stone and is finely finished. Two main temples and three smaller ones once stood in a row, east to west, with open space in between. Remains of several Saiva and Vaisnava temples are scattered round Kotitirtha tank. There is still a Siva temple in the north-west corner of the tank. On the eastern part of the fort, there are remains of some ruined temples around a tank called 'Bhurhiya-ka-Talao'. In 1990 remains of a Jain temple, the only known temple of its kind at Kalanjara, were discovered here at the eastern corner of the hill during the course of the construction of an approach road from Kalanjara to the fort.[121] The ruins of the Jain temple have yielded several Jain sculptures of Chandella period. It is significant that this is the only Jain temple in the fort exit which is in ruins.

Near the middle of the south face is the 'Mrig-dhasa' or 'Antelope's spring', a small pool in inner chamber of the rampart into which water is constantly trickling over the seven antelopes. The Puranic episode is connected with this place. There is a palace at the bank of Koti-tirtha constructed by the Bundela ruler, Aman Singh; now it is converted into a site-museum. A good collection of sculptures of Chandella period is available here. There are also numerous sculptures connected with different cults prevailing at Kalanjara.

Almost at the foot of the hill, on the north-east, there is a tank named 'Surasariganga'. This is a large tank with steps all around it, and was originally profoundly decorated with sculptures much of which still remain. It seems that there were some big temples around the tank. Near this tank, there is an image of a water-carrier, with an inscription in the Gupta script.

Thus, this description of antiquities at Kalanjara throws light on the various aspects of the Kalanjara fort. The description of Kalanjara cannot be completed without the study of art and architecture, which developed here from the Gupta period to the medieval period. Kalanjara is famous for forts, caves and structural architecture. Manu advocates the construction of forts because a single archer under the shelter of the fort wall can fight a hundred enemies and a hundred can fight ten thousand. He says that a mountain fortress is the best of all.[122] The fort of Kalanjara is a mountain fort. Due to its natural surrounding it was a very strong fort. It contains *parikha,* rampart, *gopura,* gates, *attalak* and *protli;* these were the parts of fort architecture mentioned in the architectural text. It was famous for its strength "in the whole of Hindustan" according to Muslim writers.[123] The history of the Chandella dynasty moves round this fort. It was so important that the Kalachuris assumed the title of 'Kalanjarapurvaradhisvara'. It was considered a pre-eminent town during the time of Kalachuris.[124] Similarly, Chandella rulers also assumed the title of 'Kalanjaradhipati'.[125] Muslim writers mentioned the Chandella rulers as rulers of Kalanjara.[126] We can divide the architectural remains of Kalanjara into three categories, as following:

(1) Brick architecture.
(2) Rock-cut architecture.
(3) Structural architecture.

1. Brick Architecture

Brick architecture is known from the post-Gupta inscription of Udyana discovered by Cunningham.[127] This inscription refers to the construction of the brick-temple of Bhadresvara by the Panduvamsi ruler, Udayan. The temple no longer exists, but we can know the existence of brick architecture at Kalanjara.[128]

2. Rock-cut Architecture

Rock-cut architecture started during the time of Mauryas. At Kalanjara we find several *Mukha-linga* images, Nandi bearing *Sivalinga,* Kala-Bhairava, Mahasadasiva, Visnu on Garuda, Kali and many others sculptures carved in rock near Nilakantha temple.[129]

3. Structural Architecture

At Kalanjara fort, there were several remains of temples, most of them in ruined condition. We can include fort gates, rampart, *mandapa* of Nilakantha temple, Aman Singh Palace, etc. Many Saiva, Vaisnava, Sakta and Jain images come under this category.

Thus, the study of architectural remains of Kalanjara is significant from the point of view of city architecture, fort architecture, cave architecture, temple architecture, and palace architecture.

Kalanjara is also a famous art centre. So far as art tradition is concerned, art activities started at Kalanjara as early as the pre-historic period. Many pre-historic rock-painting sites have been discovered in and around the Kalanjara region.[130]

Some interesting religious seals were unearthed by Marshall at Bhita; a good many show undoubted Saiva features; the various Saiva emblems like the *linga,* the trident-axe, the *nandipada* and the bull are clearly recognizable on them. Some of the seals bear the different names of Siva such as Kalesvara, Kalanjara-bhattaraka, Bhadresvara, Kalanjara and Mahesvara.[131] Some of these are related to Kalanjara. These seals belong to the Gupta period and throw light on the religious activities prevailing at Kalanjara during the Gupta period.

The sculptures of Kalanjara are divided into two types: rock-cut and stone sculptures. These sculptures are connected with different religious sects.

The largest number of sculptures found at Kalanjara are related to Saivism. Siva is worshipped in a number of anthropomorphic forms and in the symbols of *linga.* The more common representation is the latter one. The *linga* images from Kalanjara are broadly classified into two types: rock-cut and other.[132] A large number of *linga* images from Kalanjara are rock-cut. There are a few interesting *linga* images, which are not according to Silpa texts. In these images the artists of Kalanjara introduce their originality. At Kalanjara, on a path leading to the Nilakantha temple, among other reliefs is shown a Nandi bearing a *Sivalinga* on his back[133] while one man and two women are seated with folded hands in devotional posture. There is also an unfinished sketch on the rock which was left uncarved by the artist; it shows the process of making of rock-cut sculptures. One such image of Nandi bearing a *Sivalinga* and also having the five *linga*s on his back is in the museum collection.[134] *Mukha-linga* is one of the varities of *Manush-linga*. At Kalanjara, we find both the varieties – rock-cut and carved – on stone slabs. We find a large number of small and bigger *Mukha-linga* having one face carved on the rock. These images are not only in large numbers but also have an artistic quality in them. The other type of *linga* images found at Kalanjara are *Sahstra-linga, Panch-linga* and *Panch Mukha-linga*. These images show the popularity of *linga* worship at Kalanjara.

At Kalanjara we also find many images of Siva in human form. There are several images of Uma-Mahesvara and Bhairava, etc. There are also Natesh sculptures of Siva found at Kalanjara. Silapatta images of various deities are also carved at Kalanjara. One unique image of the nine-headed Mahasadasiva is carved near Nilakantha temple.

Thus, the art of Kalanjara furnishes valuable material for the study of the iconography of the Saiva pantheon, of the 'Panch-devas' and also the 'Vyantara-devatas'. Numerous figures of the Nagas and river goddesses have been discovered in and around Kalanjara. Similarly, numerous sculptures of Visnu, Sakti, Ganesha and Laxmi are also carved at various places in Kalanjara.

This sculptural wealth related to different cults found at Kalanjara proves that Kalanjara was the most significant centre of Chandella art.

AJAIGARH

The fort of Ajaigarh is situated in Panna district of Madhya Pradesh. It is 80 km from Khajuraho and about 30 km from Kalanjara. The fort stands on a flat-topped spur of the Vindhyan hills, within sight of the river Ken, which is only five miles distant. It is of about the same height as Kalanjara or between 700 and 800 feet above the plain. The lower part of the hill, which is of granite, is not very steep, but the upper part, which consist of reddish sandstone, is very steep. The area of the fort is nearly 1 mile in length from north to south, and only a little less from west to east. It is nearly triangular in shape, and the circuit of its walls just three miles.

The foundation of Ajaigarh is credited to an unknown ruler, Ajaypal. But the name Ajaigarh is not found in any of the inscriptions, the name being invariably given as Jayapura-durga or the 'Fortress of Jayapura'.[135] In one of the inscriptions from Ajaigarh it is referred to as 'Nandipura'[136] Two copper-plates of Maharaja Laxman were issued from 'Jayapura' discovered at Pali[137] (near Allahabad) and Singroli (near Sidhi in M.P.).[138] It seems these copper-plates belong to 'Jayapur,' which is mentioned in the Chandella inscriptions. Both the copper-plates are dated in G.E. 158 (AD 478). Thus, the antiquity of Ajaigarh goes up to the post-Gupta period.[139]

The fort has two gates, one to the north being called Darwaza, and the other to the south-east, named the Tarhowan, at the foot of the hill. In the inscriptions Cunningham finds mention of the Kalanjara-Darwaza or Kalanjara-Gate, and this must be the Darwaza on the north, as it leads towards Kalanjara.[140]

Near the northern gate there are two ponds excavated in the rock, which are locally known by the name of Ganga-Yamuna.[141] Almost exactly in the middle of the fort there is a large tank excavated in the rock called 'Ajaypal-ka-Talao'. It is evidently old but the black stone figure on the bank, which is called Ajaypal, is a statue of four-armed Visnu. Here, there are some sati pillars lying near the ruined Jain temple of Shantinatha.

Near the southern end of the fort, there in another tank called 'Parmal Tal'. Close by there is a ruined temple of the Chandella period, also associated with Parmal or Parmardi-deva, and at a short distance, there are two other temples standing together, which are locally known as 'Ranga Mahal'. There is one more temple standing nearby. These temples are in a ruined condition but they are richly decorated. Two of them are related to Visnu and one is related to Siva. The doorjambs of these temple are profusely ornamented; many sculptures of Chandella period still remain in these temples. In one of the ruined temple, there is a very artistic decoration of snakes.

On the rock at the Tarhoni Gate, there is a row of eight goddesses (the *Ashta Sakti*), of which seven are sitting and one standing. Their names are carved below.

Close by there is a long inscription of the Chandella period. There are also several rows of Jain images sitting in *padmasana*. Near these there is a cow and calf and a four-armed goddess sitting with a child in her lap, and five pigs above one another on her right side, and eight pigs in pairs above one another on her left hand side. Thus, it is evidently the figure of Shashti, the goddess of fecundity.

The antiquities of Ajaigarh fort are important for the study of art and architecture. At Ajaigarh we find both types of architecture, structural and rock-cut. Similarly, we find the images of various deities belonging to Saiva, Vaisnava, Jain and Sakti cult. The image of Dani Vinayaka is very significant. Similarly, the rock-cut image of mother and child is also important. The sculptural art of Ajaigarh also contributed a lot in Chandella art and architecture.[142] The fort of Ajaigarh is also included in the eight forts of the Chandellas. It was a seat of civil administration of the Chandellas.[143] This fort-town became a capital of the Chandellas in the declining period of their dynasty.

MAHOBA

Mahoba is a historic city of the Chandellas. It is situated at the fort of granite hill, about 80 km to the south of Hamirpur (U.P.), at the junction of the Betwa and Yamuna, and 65 km to the north of Khajuraho. The ancient name of the city was Mahotsavanagar or 'the city of the great festival'.[144] Cunningham believes that it got its name from the great festival which was celebrated there by Chandravarman, the traditional founder of the dynasty.[145] Among the surviving monuments of Mahoba, 'Kakra-Matha' occupied a rock island in the north-western corner of the Madan Sagar Lake; it is made of granite. In size, it is equal to the largest of Khajuraho temples. The sanctum is empty but the marks of a *linga* indicate its Saiva affiliation. Mahoba was also a subsidiary seat of Manyadeva, the family deity of the Chandellas who are believed to have brought his worship to Mahoba.[146] The temple dedicated to him is modern by appearance.

Mahoba is dotted with hillocks all around; whichever direction one moves around rock-cut reliefs are visible. Of most importance among these larger-than-life representations is a massive sculpture known as Gajasura-Samhara. Siva is depicted in a forceful manner. Nearby this colossal carving, we have the full family of Siva on the face of another primeval rock – the gorgeous sculptures of Gajari Siva.

Mahoba was also a centre of Jainism. At present nothing of that survives, but it did have a hold on Mahoba sculptures of *tirthankaras* like Rishabhanatha, Padmaprabhu, Neminath and Parshvanatha Mahavira, which have been shifted to Jhansi Museum. A variety of stones have been used to carve out these images.

A few rock-cut reliefs behind the temple of Badi Chandik include sculptures of *Yaksas*. A natural cave contained the figures of Adinatha, Neminatha, Parshvanatha and Yakshi Padmavati.

Mahoba was also a centre of Buddhism. Cunningham discovered the images of Buddha, Simhananda, Lokesvara, Padmapani, Avalokitesvara and Tara. These Buddhist sculptures are considered a great contribution of the Chandellas.

Saktism at Mahoba acquired considerable following. Sakti's Chamunda form had special appeal here and we meet with numerous representations of her. Most of them are rock-cut reliefs. A unique image shows the deity with sixty-four hands.[150]

Mahoba is famous for it tanks and lakes. The Chandella ruler, Rahil, constructed a large tank, named as Rahilyasagar. The Kirtisagar lake is attributed by tradition to King Kirtivarman and Madanasagar to Madanavarman. The remains of the palace of King Paramarde are believed to be located in the fort area.

Thus the remains of Mahoba also indicate that it was a centre of Chandella art and architecture.

KHAJURAHO

The Khajuraho temples constitute the highest achievement of the sculpture and architectural art of medieval central India. Erotic sculpture are not the only attraction of Khajuraho. This magnificent site of temples was recognised as a world heritage site by the UNESCO in 1986. Adding to the attraction of these temples, there are several historical and natural sites of great scenic beauty in the surroundings of Khajuraho.

Khajuraho (Latitude: 24° 51′ N, Longitude: 79° 56′ E), situated in the Chhatarpur district of Madhya Pradesh, preserves the largest and most magnificent groups of Chandella temples. It is situated on the banks of Khudar Nala, a tributary of Ken River. The area is surrounded by water-falls and hills of the Vindhya range, which provide an attractive backdrop to the temple complex.

According to local tradition, the place had eighty-five temples,[147] but only twenty-five now remain in different stages of preservation. There are more than fifty mounds at Khajuraho, of which eighteen have been identified for future excavation. Recently, a beautiful carved plinth of a large, early eleventh century temple was unearthed in the southern area of the site.[148]

The earliest drawings of Khajuraho were made in 1852 by F.C. Maisey.[149] The first systematic description of Khajuraho was given by Cunningham, in *Archaeological Survey of Indian Reports*, Volumes II, VII, X and XXI, which are a rich source of information on this site. He recognised its importance and said that the area contains perhaps the largest group of costly Hindu temples that are now to be found in northern India.[150]

The most significant feature of the Khajuraho temples is that they are connected with different sects existing at Khajuraho those days. Of the twenty-five temples existing today, ten enshrine Vishnu in his various forms. Eight are dedicated to Siva, one to Surya, one to sixty-four *yoginis* while five are Jain temples.

The Khajuraho temples are divided into three parts:

(1) The Western Group, consisting of the following parts:
(i) Devi, (ii) Varaha, (iii) Lakshmana, (iv) Kandariya Mahadeva, (v) Mahadeva, (vi) Devi Jagadamba, (vii) Chitragupta, (viii) Parvati, (ix) Matangesvara, (x) Chausath-yogini, (xi) Bhagwan Mahadeva.

(2) The Eastern Group, consisting of the following temples:
(i) Brahma, (ii) Vamana, (iii) Javari, (iv) Parshvanatha, (v) Adinatha, (vi) Shantinath temple, (vi) Ghantai.

(3) Southern Group, consisting of the following temples:
(i) Duladeva, (ii) Chaturbhuja, (iii) Bijamandala temple.[151]

Now Chandella sculptures need a re-classification, because the previous classification was based on Khajuraho alone. Chandella sculptures may firstly be divided into two parts, viz.,

(1). Stone sculptures
(2). Rock-cut sculptures

The stone sculptures were carved by sculptors on the stone slabs brought by the labourers from nearby stone quarries. The stone sculptures were mostly the component of temple architecture in Chandella art. Sculptures of this type are classified by Krishna Deva[152] into five categories.

The first category comprises formal cult-images executed almost completely in the round, in strict conformity with textual formulae and prescriptions.[153] These images lack aesthetic expressions, and they are generally carved in standing posture.

The second category comprises *parivara, parsva* and *avaranadevata*s. These sculptures are carved in the niches or are figured against the walls of temples and are executed either in round or in high or medium relief. Sculptures occurring in the niches are more formal and partake of iconographic qualities of the cult image of the first category. The remaining figures are of gods and goddesses, which include those of 'Dik-palas', the less formal and more free. These usually stand in attractive *tribhanga* and are distinguished from humans only by their particular head-dress or mounts or special attributes held usually in more than two hands.[154] The third category of the sculptures consists of the *apsara*s or *sura-sundari*s, who account for the finest and most numerous sculptures in Chandella art, executed either in round or in high or medium relief on the outer or inner walls, pillars and ceilings. The *apsara*s are invariably represented as beautiful and youthful nymphs, attired in choicest gems and dresses and full of winsome grace and charm. As heavenly dancers they are shown dancing in various postures. As attendants of higher divinities, they are represented with folded hands or carrying the lotus flower, mirrors, water-jar, raiments, ornaments, etc., as offerings for deities.[155] But more frequently, the *sura-sundari*s are portrayed to express common human moods, emotions and activities and are often difficult to distinguish from conventional *nayaka*s.[156] Such *apsara*s are shown as disrobing, yawning, scratching the back, touching the breast, rinsing water from the wet plaits of hair, removing thorns, fondling a baby, playing with pets like parrots and monkey, and designing the wall or bedecking themselves in various ways by painting the feet, applying collyrium, etc.[157] The *apsara*s are also found at Kalanjara, Ajaigarh and some other places of Chandella art. The *apsara*s of Khajuraho are the best creation of Chandella art.

The fourth category consists of secular sculptures which comprise various themes, including domestic life scenes, comprising teacher and disciples, dancers and musicians, and erotic couples or groups. The last include some of the finest sculptural compositions of Chandella art, vibrating with rare sensitiveness and warmth of human emotion.[158]

The fifth category is of sculptured animals, including the Vyala or Sardula, which is heraldic and a fabulous animal, primarily represented as a rampant horned lion with a player attacking it from behind. Different varieties of this basic type are known with heads of elephants, men, parrots, boars, etc. Like *apsara*s, this most typical and popular sculptural theme of Chandella art is similarly related with deep symbolism.[159] The Chandella artist also depicted the royal hunt, different types of animals, birds, reptiles and others for decorative purposes. We find a beautiful ornamental decoration of snakes at Ajaigarh fort temple.[160] A rich fauna and flora finds place in Chandella art.

The second part of Chandella sculptural art consists of rock-cut sculptures, which are less studied by art historians. They are over-shadowed by the charm of the magnificent temple sculpture of Khajuraho. The rock-cut sculptures were carved at Ajaigarh, Kalanjara, Mahoba and Deogarh. In these sculptures, we find the development of rock-cut art tradition of Udaygiri (Vidisa). The Chandella artist utilised the rocks for construction of temples, caves, tanks, lakes, and ponds, and various types of sculptures related to different religions prevalent during the Chandella period were carved. We find the cult image of Siva, Visnu, Sakti and Jain *tirthankara*s carved out in rocks at various places.[161] At Kalanjara fort, there were many small and bigger *Mukha-linga* images carved out in rocks near the Nilakantha temple. A unique, large Mahabhairava or Kala-Bhairava image was carved by the Chandella artist during the time of Paramardideva. It is even mentioned in the *Ain-i-Akbari*.[162] The portrait type rock-cut images of Mirki-Bhairava and Bhairavi are the unique rock-cut sculptures found at Kalanjara.[165] The unique nine-headed Mahasadasiva image near Nilakantha temple is also a rare creation of the Chandella artist at Kalanjara. Somepatta sculptures are also carved at Kalanjara, which are very significant for the study of composite form of worship.[164] The characteristic feature of these is that they are independent and not a part of temple architecture.

Chandella art is very significant for the study of iconography. The Chandella temples were dedicated to Visnu, Siva, Surya, Sakti and the *tirthankara*s. The artists have carved some rare images of these divinities, which express deep philosophical concepts that the Chandella rulers were worshippers of Visnu. Visnu is associated with royalty and regal power. All his ten incarnations are represented in Chandella art. An inscription from Ajaigarh describes all the incarnations.[165] The Varaha, Vamana and Narasimha incarnations of Visnu were popular in Chandella region. Vaikuntha, a composite form with faces of Varaha and a lion with human face, was installed in a temple at Khajuraho by the Chandella Yasovarman.[166] The other incarnations represented in Chandella art are Matsya, Kurma, Narasimha, Parasurama, Rama, Balarama, Krishna, Buddha and Kalki. Among the rare images at Khajuraho are those of Visnu as Yogesvara, seated in *padmasana*, giving discourse to sages placed in upper cardinal niche of the Lakshman temple. Visnu making a gesture of silence with four fingers near his lips is one unique sculpture not found anywhere else in Indian art.[167] The scene of 'Krishna lila' in different forms is also depicted in Chandella art.[168] The exchange of babies' scene is rare in Chandella art, depicted in a pillar at Kalanjara.[169]

Both the placid and terrific manifestations of Siva are represented in Chandella art. These are Natesh, Kalyanasundar, Ardhanarisvara, Uma-Mahesvara, Andhakasvaravadha, Tripurantaka, Bhairava and others.

The most important is the Sadasiva image of Siva from Khajuraho, depicting him with four feet. This four-legged image of Sadasiva metaphorically suggests the four parts of the text of the Saiva-Siddhanta sect, associated with the Chandellas.[170]

Various forms of *linga* images of Siva are also depicted and installed in the Siva temples. At Kalanjara we find unique *linga* images of seated Nandi bearing a *Sivalinga* or *Panchalinga*s.[171] There is a fairly good number of images of divine couples like Indra and Sachi, Uma-Mahesvara, Brahma-Saraswati, Kama and Rati, Kuber and Ridhi, Ganesh and Vigneswari, Laxmi-Narayana, Balarama-Ravati, Rama-Sita and Agni-Swaha.[172] These divine couple images are also in bigger number and we do not find such a depiction elsewhere in Indian art.

The integrated study of Chandella art reveals that it has made a unique contribution in medieval Indian art and befittingly the Khajuraho temples have been considered as world heritage site by the UNESCO. The Chandella forts and other sites are worth studying from the point of view of art development and their contribution is equally significant.

NOTES AND REFERENCES

1. R.K. Dikshit, *Chandellas of Jejakabhukti*, Preface, p. vi.
2. *Epigraphia Indica*, Vol. , pp. 325-30.
3. *Purmal Raso*, Book II, Vs. 28 & 54.
4. Devangana Desai, *Khajuraho*, p. 8; *Chandellas of Jejakabhukti*, pp. 10-11.
5. *Journal of Asiatic Society of Bengal* (1895), p. 38.
6. *Epigraphia Indica*, Vol. 1, p. 47.
7. R.K. Dikshit, *op. cit.*, p. 12, fn. 3.
8. *Ibid.*, p. 11; *Religious Imagery of Khajuraho*, p. 38.
9. *Ramayana* (Gita Press), 11,-94.
10. *Journal of Indian History*, No. 136, p. 34, fn. 2.
11. S.D. Trivedi, *Bundelkhand Ka Puratattava*, pp. 10-11.
12. Krishna Deva, *Khajuraho*, p. 3.
13. R.N. Mishra, *Bhartiya Murti Kala*, p. 54.
14. Krishna Deva, *op. cit.*, p. 3.
15. *Marg*, 26, No. 3, p. 47.
16. Krishna Deva, *op. cit.*, p. 3.
17. *Ibid.*
18. *Ibid.*
19. *Ibid.*, p. 10.
20. *Ibid.*
21. N.S. Bose, *History of the Chandellas*, p. 13.
22. R.K. Dikshit, *op. cit.*, p. 15.
23. *Ibid.*
24. N.S. Bose, *op. cit.*, p. 13.
25. Cunningham, *Archaeological Survey of India*, Reports, Vol. XXI, p. 78.
26. N.S. Bose, *op. cit.*, p. 172.
27. S.K. Sullerey, 'Chandella Historiography', *Journal of the Asiatic Society of Mumbai*, Vols. 77, 78.
28. S.K. Sullerey, *Chandella Art*, p. 22.
29. S.K. Sullerey, *Ajaigarh Aur Kalanjara Ki Devapratimayain*, pp. 7, 29.
30. D.L. Drake-Brockman, *Banda, A Gazetteer*, p. 239.
31. *Ibid.*
32. B.N. Roy, *Kalanjara a Historical and Cultural Profile*, p. 1.
33. A. Cunningham, *op. cit.*, Vol. XXI, p. 22.
34. *Ibid.*
35. *Ibid.*
36. *Ibid.* p. 91.
37. *Imperial Gazetteer of India*, pp. 310-11.
38. *Mahabharata* (Pune Edn.) 3/83/53 – 3/85/13 – 15; 13/26/33.
39. *Ibid.*, 3/85/13-15.
40. *Ibid.*, 13/26/33.
41. Valmiki, *Ramayana*, 7/2/39.
42. S.K. Sullerey, *Ajaigarh Aur Kalanjara Ke Devapratimayain*, p. 9.
43. *Archaeological Survey of India, Annual Report*, 1911-12, p. 49.
44. *Ibid.*
45. J.N. Banerjea, *The Development of Hindu Iconography*, pp. 182-184.

46. *Ibid.*
47. *Ibid.*
48. V.S. Pathak suggested this reading after seeing this inscription.
49. S.K. Sullerey, *Ajaigarh Aur Kalanjara Ke Devapratimayain*, p. 10.
50. A. Cunningham, *op. cit.*, Vol. XXI, p. 21-22.
51. *Padma Purana* (Bhumikhand), 91, 39, 92, 1.
52. *Brahma Purana*, 2/46/1.
53. *Garuda Purana*, 81/18/19.
54. *Padma Purana*, 90/34.
55. *Skanda Purana*, 14/6/25.
56. A. Cunningham, *op. cit.*, Vol. XXI, p. 28.
57. *Garuda Purana*, 81/18/19.
58. *Padma Purana*, 81/18, 38/15.
59. *Agni Purana*, 109/21.
60. *Brahma Purana*, 2/146/1.
61. *Matsya Purana*, 32/109.
62. *Vayu Purana*, 77/93.
63. *Brahmanda Purana*, 3/13/100.
64. *Vayu Purana*, 23/104.
65. *Linga Purana*, 24/104.
66. *Kurma Purana*, 36/35-38.
67. *Vaman Purana*, 90/27.
68. *Epigraphia Indica*, Vol. 1, pp. 27-28, V. 31.
69. *Ibid.*, Vol. XXX, pp. 87-90.
70. A. Cunningham, *op. cit.*, Vol. XXI, p. 34.
71. *Ibid.*, pp. 33 to 45.
72. *Padma Purana*, 17/196.
73. *Matsya Purana*, 13/32.
74. *Devi Bhagvat Purana*, 30/62/-38/39.
75. *Harivamsa Purana*, 1/21-24-27; 1/20/25.
76. *Agni Purana*, 117/55.
77. *Padma Purana*, 47/302, 10/96-63; *Agni Purana*, 117/55.
78. *Sacred Book of East*, Part 57, fn. 3.
79. *Ibid.*
80. A. Cunningham, *op. cit.*, Vol. XXI, p. 31.
81. *Ibid.*, Vol. XXI, p. 23.
82. *Imperial Gazetteer of India*, Part, XIV, pp. 310-13.
83. S.K. Mitra, *Early Ruler of Khajuraho*, p. 24.
84. *Epigraphia Indica*, Vol. 1, p. 127-28, V. 31.
85. N.S. Bose, *op. cit.*, p. 172.
86. *Ibid.*
87. *Ibid.*, p. 44.
88. *I.A.*, Vol. XV, pp. 36, 41, Vs. 6.
89. R.C. Majumdar, *Ancient India*, p. 351.
90. S.K. Sullerey, *Ajaigarh Aur Kalanjara Ki Devapratimayain*, p. 63.
91. H.C. Ray, *Dynastic History of Northern India*, Vol. II, p. 693.
92. A. Cunningham, *op. cit.*, Vol. XXI, pp. 28-29.
93. N.S. Bose, *op. cit.*, p. 44.
94. R.C. Majumdar (ed.), *Classical Age*, pp. 220-21.
95. *Ibid.*, *Struggle for Empire*, p. 179.
96. *Epigraphia Indica*, Vol. XX, p. 18.
97. *Ibid.*, Vol. 1, pp. 127-28.

98. A. Cunningham, *op. cit.*, Vol. XXI, p. 28.
99. *Ibid.*
100. *Ibid.*, pp. 33 ff.
101. *Ibid.*, pp. 20 ff.
102. *Ibid.*, p. 28 ff.
103. *Ibid.*, pp. 28-29.
104. *Ibid.*, p. 29.
105. Reading of Prof. V.S. Pathak.
106. A. Cunningham, *op. cit.*, Vol. XXI, p. 30.
107. *Ibid.*
108. *Ibid.*
109. *Ibid.*
110. *Ibid.*
111. *A.S.I.A.R.*, 1935-36, p. 93.
112. Gopinath Rao, *Elements of Hindu Iconography*, Vol. II, p. 79.
113. *Ibid.*
114. *Vaman Purana*, 90, 27.
115. *Epigraphia Indica*, Vol. I, pp. 127-28.
116. A. Cunningham, *op. cit.*, Vol. XXI, p. 34.
117. *Ibid.*, pp. 37-38.
118. *Ibid.*, pp. 33 ff.
119. *A.S.I.A.R.*, 1935-36, p. 93.
120. A. Cunningham, *op. cit.*, Vol. XXI, p. 33.
121. B.N. Roy, *Kalanjara – A Cultural Profile*, p. 52.
122. Manu, VIII, 74.
123. A. Cunningham, *op. cit.*, Vol. XXI, p. 24.
124. *Epigraphia Indica*, Vol. VII, pp. 85-93.
125. N.S. Bose, *op. cit.*, p. 44.
126. Briggs Firishta, Part I, p. 18.
127. A. Cunningham, *op. cit.*, Vol. XXI, p. 29.
128. Prof. V.S. Pathak's reading.
129. S.K. Sullerey, *Ajaigarh Aur Kalanjara Ki Devapratimayain*, p. 23-24.
130. B.N. Roy, *Kalanjara – A Cultural Profile*, p. 8.
131. J.N. Benerja, *Development of Hindu Iconography*, pp. 182, 184.
132. S.K. Sullerey, *Chandella Art*, p. 31.
133. *Ibid.*, p. 34.
134. *Ibid.*
135. A. Cunningham, *op. cit.*, Vol. XXI, p. 46.
136. *Epigraphia Indica*, Vol. I, pp. 325-30.
137. *Ibid.*, Vol. II, p. 364.
138. *A.S.I.A.R.*, 1936-37, p. 88.
139. S.K. Sullerey, *Ajaigarh Aur Kalanjara Ki Devapratimayain*, p. 34.
140. A. Cunningham, *op. cit.*, Vol. XXI, p. 47.
141. *Ibid.*
142. S.K. Sullerey, *Chandella Art*, p. 34.
143. N.S. Bose, *op. cit.*, p. 135.
144. *Ibid.*, p. 13.
145. *Ibid.*
146. A.P. Pandey, *Chandella Kalin Bundelkhand*, p. 96.
147. *Parmal Raso*, Book II, Vs., 28 & 54.
148. Devangana Desai, *Khajuraho*, p. 6.
149. *Ibid.*, p. 4.

150. A. Cunningham, Vol. XXI, Preface, p. iii.
151. Devangana Desai, *op. cit.*, pp. 49 ff.
152. S.K. Sullerey, *Chandella Art*, p. 32.
153. *Ibid.*
154. *Ibid.*
155. Krishna Deva, *op. cit.*, p. 14.
156. *Ibid.*
157. *Ibid.*
158. *Ibid.*
159. *Ibid.*, p. 15.
160. S.K. Sullerey, *Chandella Art*, p. 34.
161. *Ibid.*
162. A. Cunningham, *op. cit.*, Vol. XXI, p. 33.
163. S.K. Sullerey, *Chandella Art*, p. 34.
164. *Ibid.*
165. *Epigraphia Indica*, Vol. XXXIII, pp. 98-107.
166. Devangana Desai, *op. cit.*, p. 41.
167. *Ibid.*
168. Krishna Deva, *op. cit.*, pp. 121-106.
169. S.K. Sullerey, *Chandella Art*, p. 35.
170. Devangana Desai, *op. cit.*, p. 43.
171. S.K. Sullerey, *Chandella Art*, p. 36.
172. *Ibid.*

3

Geographical Environment

The word environment is derived from the French 'environ'.[1] Environment can be defined as the physical and biological world that surrounds us, as well as the complex of social and cultural conditions affecting an individual or community. This definition includes both the natural world and 'built' environment, as well as the cultural and social contexts that shape human lives. Historically, environment is rooted in natural history, a search for beauty and meaning in nature. Modern environmental sciences expand this concern, drawing on every area of humanities and physical sciences. Its strongest roots, however, are in ecology, the study of interrelationship among organisms and their physical environment.[2]

The Jejakabhukti region of present Uttar Pradesh and Madhya Pradesh comprises of four dictricts of Chitrakuta Division (Banda, Chhatrapati Shahuji Maharaj Nagar (Chitrakuta), Hamirpur and Mahoba); three disctricts of Jhansi (Jalaun, Jhansi and Lalitpur); five districts of Sagar Division (Panna, Chhatarpur, Damoh, Tikamgarh and Sagar); and one district of Gwalior Division (Datia). During the Chandella period, Gwalior was also a part of Chandella kingdom. The study of geographical environment is of great significance, its relevance on creativity is too much. The region occupied by the Chandellas owing to its unique geographical location between the north and south part of India, its hilly surroundings and its natural resources has attracted kings and sages alike through the ages. The region played an important role in the political and cultural life of our country. The place has been endowed with beautiful mountains, good perennial rivers, fast flowing seasonal rivulets, thick and large forest areas with traditional timber, tendu and herbal plants and rich fertile plains. According to local traditions, it contained the *ashramas* (hermitages) of famous *rishis* as Valmiki, Vedavyasa, Atri and Agastya.[3] The region is very rich in its natural resources and remarkable for its beautiful scenery, which even attracted the attention of Rama[4] during his exile. It is located on the northern spur of the Vindhyan mountain. This holy *tirtha,* the abode of the gods, is set in sylvan surroundings of the beautiful river Mandakini. The name of Chitrakuta also indicates the hill of rock paintings. Many rock paintings have been discovered near Chitrakuta. Chitrakuta and Kalanjara have been included in the holy *tirthas* from ancient times.[5]

Geographical environment has played a significant role in all spheres of creative arts during the Chandella period. The detailed instructions are given in the architectural texts regarding the selection of the site for construction of forts, towns and temples.[6]

Generally the site should have plenty of water, trees and groves. Thus, the spots best suited for construction of temples were those skirted by forests, rivers, mountains and cataracts. But in the densely populated cities and towns where natural scenery is conspicuous by its absence the selected site compensated for the absence by laying out gardens and parks, for the presence of gods was considered to be easy of access in those places alone which are furnished with water and gardens, natural or artificial. 'Deities,' according to Varahamihira, comes near the spots furnished with water and groves, natural or artificial. The gods are delighted to dwell in places skirted by forests, rivers, mountains and cataract as also furnished with parks.[7]

> The gods always play where lakes are, where the sun's rays are warded off by umbrellas of lotus leads clusters, and where clear water paths are made by swans whose breast toss the white lotuses hither and thither, where swans, ducks, curleys and paddy birds are heard and animals rest nearby in the shade of Nicula trees on the river banks.[8]

The gods always reside where rivers have for their bracelets, the sound of the flight of curleys and the voice of swans for their speech, water as their garment, craps for their zone, the flowering trees on their banks as earrings, the confluence of rivers as their hips, raised sand banks as breasts and the plumage of swans as their mantle.[9] The gods always reside where groves are near rivers, mountains and springs and in towns with pleasure gardens.[10]

The images of gods are installed not only in *tirtha*s, on the banks of rivers, lakes and on the sea shores, of the confluence of rivers and estuaries, but also on hill-tops and mountain slopes, in forests, groves and gardens, near the abodes blest or hermitages, in villages, towns and cities or in any other lovely place.[11] The site of the temple is a *tirtha* where it is situated.[12] The *Visnudharmottara Purana* refers of the installation of consecrated images thus:

> Installation should be made in forts, in auspicious cities, at the head of shop-lined streets, in villages or hamlets of cowherds where there are no shops, the installation should be made outside in gardens, installation should be made at riverside, in forests, gardens, at the side of ponds, on hill tops, in beautiful villages and particularly in caves. At these places, the denizens of heaven are present.

A temple therefore should be built where there is a pond on the left, or in front and not otherwise. If a temple is built on an island, the water on all sides is auspicious.[13] Almost all the Chandella temples, ruined or existing, are thus found to have tanks or other water sources near them.[14] The practice of artificially making a site suitable by making a temple was a very early custom with the Chandellas. It is therefore very probable that the artist did not stop with merely the excavation of a tank or the foundation of a garden by the side of the temple, to make it attractive to the gods, but also carved on the temples themselves scenes from nature. Creepers and foliages, peacocks and swans, herds of elephants and monkeys are the favourite elements of all the temples in Chandella art and architecture. A reference in the *Samarangana Sutradhara,*[15] of the figures to be carved on temples, points to these facts. This tendency of making the site attractive according to the injunctions of the *Silpasastra*s is apparent from the texts as well as the decorations of the temples themselves.[16]

KALANJARA

Kalanjara, which became the site of one of the famous forts of India,[17] was widely known since past several centuries as an abode of Nilakantha Siva.[18] According to Wilson, it is mentioned in the Vedas as one of the 'Tapasyasthana'.[19] The antiquity of Kalanjara is also testified by the epics and *Puranas*.[20] The name of Kalanjara is said to have been derived from 'Siva' himself, who as 'Kala' causes all things responsible for decay (*jara*) and, therefore, destroyer of all things. He is god of death.[21] The ascetics of Kalanjara have been devoted to the worship of Siva.[22] Thus, Kalanjara has been a centre of Saivism from earliest times. It is also considered an important *tirtha* in the epics[23] and Puranas.[24] Kalanjara is situated in the midst of Vindhyan forest (Vindhyatavi).[25] It attracted the attention of ancient sages, who found the place very congenial for penances. This indicates the sancity of the hill of Kalanjara as a resort of holy ascetics. The overhanging rocks of Kalanjara provided shelter to *rishis*, and the rainwater percolating through the rocks from above gave them water to drink. The beautiful natural environment of Kalanjara was also very ideal for penances. There are many sculptures at Kalanjara depicting ascetics in various postures at several places.[26] We find the depiction of several inscribed images of ascetics carved below the ceiling of the sanctum. The Kalanjara inscription of AD 1090 belonging to the reign of Chandella ruler Kirtivarman records the construction of a *mandapa* for the temple of Nilakantha by Srimurti, the Guru of the king, and also mentions the Saivas and Pasupatas.[27] This clearly indicates the presence of Saiva-Siddharta ascetics in Kalanjara. The same inscription from Kalanjara described the Ganga as foliage banner fluttering on the pillar, that is, Siva along with Parvati as Salabhanjika.[28] This description gives a very beautiful expression of environmental effect on the composition of the inscription and also gives a decorative motif to artists. Kalanjara is not associated only with Saivism, but it is also associated with other cults prevalent during the time of the Chandellas.[29] There is a good amount of description in Puranic literature which indicates the different aspects of religious life at Kalanjara.[30] Thus, the geographical environment of Kalanjara turned the place into a 'tirtha' and then Khestra[31] connecting it with various religious cults.[32]

Owing to the geographical location and strategic position, Kalanjara transformed as a famous fort of India.[33] According to a Muslim writer, the fort of Kalanjara has no equal in the whole of the country of Hindustan for strength and impregnability.[34] As to when it changed as a fort is a matter of controversy. According to Cunningham, it seems highly probable that the fortress of Kalanjara may have been founded at least as early as the beginning of the Christian era.[35] Fort, one of the seven constituents of a state, represents the defensive power. Kamandaka rightly defines *Durg* (fort) as that which is meant for carrying on Tusni warfare which affords protection to the people, which can overpower friends and foes alike, and which is a check against the attacks of the neighbouring power and forest tribes."[36] This definition sums up very precisely the nature and significance of the Kalachuri-Chandella forts. The importance attributed to the foothills was undoubtedly due to the frequency and nature of warfare in early medieval India. The fort provided shelter and security to the royalty and their treasure and army, as well as to the subjects and allies.[37] It was not easy to capture a king entrenched within the walls of his castle and he was therefore advised to seek shelter within it when assailed by a more powerful adversary.[38] Naturally enough, a ruler who possessed a large number of forts and strongholds commanded the respect not only of his own people but also of his enemies.[39] Kautilya advised the construction of forts and establishment of the capital in one of them. He says that in the four quarters of the boundaries of the kingdom, forts should be built for offering resistance to the enemy on ground naturally for the purpose.[40]

The geographical environment of the Jejakabhukti region influenced the history and strategy during the Chandella period. With the growth of feudal conditions, the number of hill forts and fortresses had considerably increased in the Jejakabhukti region under the Chandellas. The Ajaigarh rock inscription of Chandella ruler Viravarman provides significant information and praises King Trailokyavarman as a creator in providing strong places.[41] A minister of Chandella ruler Kirtivarman is recorded to have built the fort of Kirtigiri.[42] According to the tradition, eight forts ascribed to the Chandellas are Barigarh, Kalanjara, Ajaigarh, Maniyagarh, Murpha, Maudha, Garha and Mahiyar.[43] Of these eight forts only Kalanjara and Ajaigarh (Jayapuradurga) are mentioned in Chandella inscriptions.[44] R.S. Sharma has given a survey of fortified sites in Chandella dominion.[45] S.K. Mitra has given a list of twenty-one *Skandhavars* (Royal Camps)[46] of which many have been forts and fortress. The hill fort of Kalanjara is the most famous and important fort of India and also a military, religious, cultural and art centre of Chandella period.[47]

From the later Gupta period to the late medieval period, Kalanjara developed as a religious, political and art centre of significance. During the rule of the Panduvamsi ruler, Udayan, we have an inscriptional reference of the construction of the brick temple of Bhadresvar.[48] Similarly, Jalhana's *Suktimuktavali* mentions a king of Kalanjara named Bhimata, who composed five plays of which *Swapanadasanana* was considered the best.[49] The Kalachuris of Kalyana assumed the epithet 'Kalanjarapuravaradhisvara' (Lord of the best town of Kalanjara).[50] Thus, during the time of Kalachuris of Kalanjara it took the shape of the finest town of the region.[51] During this period, the Kalachuris were uprooted from Kalanjara, but still they took pride in assuming the above title. After the Kalachuris, it was subjugated by the Gurjar-Pratihasa of Kanauj.[52] During the reign of the Pratiharas, Kalanjara became an important 'Mandala' and the centre of their political activities during that period.[53] Several rulers of these dynasties contributed greatly to the enhancement and development of art and culture at Kalanjara.

The traditional stories give the credit for the construction of the Kalanjara fort to Chandravarman, the traditional founder of Chandella dynasty.[54] But these informations of traditional stories are not confirmed by inscriptional sources. The Khajuraho inscription of Dhanga informs us that the Chandella ruler Yasovarman captured this fort for the first time.[55] This was a great achievement for Yasovarman which enhanced the power and prestige of Chandellas. It was also signified by the assumption of the epithet 'Kalanjaradhipati' by the Chandella ruler from the time of Dhanga Chandella.[56] The Chandella ruler Vidhyadhara was the greatest and most powerful ruler of this dynasty, who effectively checked the triumphal career of Sultan Mahmud and saved his kingdom from destruction by the ruthless conqueror.[57] The sturdy fort of Kalanjara played a vital role in protecting the Chandella kingdom and temples of Khajuraho[58] due to its geographical location. During the rule of the Chandellas, Kalanjara developed as a power centre and also as a centre of art and cultural activities. During this period, Kalanjara reached its zenith in every sphere of life and prestige. The Chandella rulers were mentioned by Muslim writers as the rulers of Kalanjara.[59] An inscription from Kalanjara referred to the worship of Nilakantha (Siva) by Maha Pratihara Sangrama Simha and Maha Nachni Padmavati.[60] This reference indicates that dance and music were performed in the temple during the Chandella period. These were the past of religious activities.

Due to the environmental and geographical condition of Kalanjara, there developed a different kind of architecture. We can classify the architectural remains of Kalanjara into the following parts:

1. Civil architecture
2. Religious architecture

Civil Architecture

The civil architecture remains at Kalanjara can also be divided into two parts:

(i) Town Planning

The famous town of Kalanjara occupied a place of considerable importance in the cities of ancient India. It was such an important town that the Kalachuris assumed the title of 'Kalanjarapuravardhisvasa'.[61] It was considered the finest town during the time of the

Kalachuris. Similarly, the Chandella rulers also took pride in assuming the titles of 'Kalanjaradhipati'.[62] Muslim writers described the Chandellas as rulers of Kalanjara.[63] The town of Kalanjara is situated at the foot of the hill. It contains many remains of ramparts and three gates are the significant part of town planning. The location of these city gates are sufficiently indicated by their names, the Kamata (Chitrakuta) Gate lying to the north, the Panna Gate to the south-west, and Rewa Gate to the south-east of the town.[64]

(ii) Fort

The fort of Kalanjara is a mountain fort. Due to its geographical and environmental setting, it was a very strong and impregnable fort of India. It contains all the parts of a fort, which are mentioned in Shilpa texts such as *parikha*, rampart (*prakara*), *gopura*, gates, *attalaka* and *pratoli*. It also contains palaces, temples, caves, tanks and sculptures. This fort was famous for its strength in the whole of Hindustan, according to Muslim writers.[65]

The architectural remains of Kalanjara fort can be divided into three following categories: (i) Brick architecture, (ii) Rock-cut architecture, and (iii) Structural architecture.

(i) **Brick architecture** is known from the inscription of Udyana discovered at Kalanjara.[66] This inscription mentions the construction of a brick temple of Bhadresvara by Panduvamsi king, Udayan.[67] The temple does not exist at present.

(ii) **Rock-cut architecture**: At Kalanjara we find several rock-cut caves, ponds and tanks. The famous Nilakantha temple is also a cave temple.

(iii) **Structural architecture:** We find several remains of ruined structural temples at Kalanjara. They include fort gates, ramparts, *mandapa* of Nilakantha temple, Aman Singh Palace, etc.

Thus, the study of architectural antiquities of Kalanjara is important from the point of view of fort architecture, town architecture, cave architecture, temple architecture and palace architecture.

Kalanjara is also an important art centre. So far as art activities are concerned, they started from pre-historic period. Several pre-historic rock-painting sites have been discovered in and around Kalanjara.[68] Sculptural art of Kalanjara is divided into two types, rock-cut and stone sculptures. These sculptures are connected with different religious cults. Since Kalanjara was the main centre of Saivism, the biggest number of sculptures found at Kalanjara are related to Saivism. The art of Kalanjara furnishes valuable material for the study of the iconography of different cult images.[69] Thus, the sculptural wealth related to different cults found at Kalanjara proves that this was the most important centre of art during the Chandella period.

Thus, due to geographical environment, different aspects of Kalanjara had been developed during different periods. It is still considered a place of pilgrimage.

AJAIGARH

The fortress of Ajaigarh is situated in the Panna district of Madhya Pradesh. It is about 35 km from Panna, 80 km from Khajuraho and about 30 km from Kalanjara. It stands on a lofty, flat-topped spur of the Vindhyan hills, within the site of river Kiyan or Ken, which is about 12 km away. The lower part of the hill is not very steep, but the higher part is very abrupt and quite inaccessible to attackers.[70] The name of Ajaigarh is not found in any of the inscriptions, the name being invariably given as 'Jayapura durga' or the 'fortress of Jayapura'.[71] In one of the inscriptions from Ajaigarh fort, it is referred to as 'Nandipura'.[72] This name indicates that Ajaigarh was also related to Saivism. Ajaigarh is not mentioned as a 'tirtha'.

After the fall of Kalanjara in AD 1202, Ajaigarh became the capital of the Chandellas, and even after the recapture of Kalanjara by Trailokyavarman, some time before AD 1205, the Chandellas did not transfer their capital to Kalanjara again.[73] The whole history of the Chandellas has centred round the historic fort of Kalanjara and, to a lesser degree, the fort of Ajaigarh.[74] This extraordinary significance of forts in the Chandella kingdom was due to the geographical environment of the region and the method of warfare followed in that period.[75] The fort of Ajaigarh was also a sturdy fort; during the later period it played a significant role in the history of the Chandellas. The epigraphs found in Ajaigarh belong mainly to the later period of Chandella history after the occupation of Mahoba and Kalanjara by the Muhammadans.[76] The latest historical records at Kalanjara belong to the reign of Parmaradi Deva. But at Ajaigarh we have the earliest inscription of Kirtivarman. The series continued again from Madanavarman by one inscription of Trailokyavarman, the son of Paramaradi, followed by three of his grandson Viravarman I, two of his great grandson Bhojavarman and one grandson's grandson Viravarman II. Various inscriptions at Ajaigrah fort suggest that this place was an important seat of Chandella administration during the later period. Inscriptions from Ajaigarh show that the officer controlling the forts was appointed by the Chandella rulers. Inscriptions also record the construction of Siroitha by Jauna Pala for the use of all people in the fort of Jayapura, in the year AD 1151.[77] Similarly, another inscription at Ajaigarh fort informs us about the construction of a *bauli* (well) during the time of famine by the Vera in the year AD 1180 in the fort of Jayapura for the use of all people.[78] This inscription is significant from the point of view of relief works also being carried out during the time of the Chandellas. In another inscription, there is similar information of the constructions of *Chautra* by the Sri Sinhad for use of common people in the fort of Jayapura in the year AD 1186.[79] All the above-mentioned construction works were carried out by the persons residing in the village Kotia. This village is not identified till now; it must be located near Ajaigarh fort.

Ajaigarh rock inscriptions of the time of Kirtivarman inform us about the worship of Chandika. Its object is to eulogise Jajuka and Maheshwar, the scions of a Vastavya Kayastha family that served the Chandellas with great devotion and distinction. The former is said to have bestowed 'Jagati patitvam' upon King Ganda and received the village of Dugauda in reward. The latter, who had rendered meritorious services to Kirtivarman while he was in distress in the region of Pitadri, was granted the village of Pipalahika. He was also placed in charge of the gates of the fort of Kalanjara. This inscription also traced the origin of the Vastavya family from Brahma's Sonkasyapa.[80] This inscription further gives us information regarding an important hill named Pitadri.

At Ajaigarh fort this stone inscription is inscribed on a block of rockstone, bearing an image of Ganesha in relief. This inscription mentions Lakshmidhara, Yashapala, Sridhara, Gokula, Bhoja, Mahipal, Gangadhara and Jagadhara, belonging to a Gauda family, who had served in responsible positions under Chandella kings Kiritivarman, Sallaksanavarman, Jayavarman, Prithvivarman, Madanavarman, Paramardin, Trailokyavarman and Viravarman. The object of the inscription is to record that Ganadhisa or Ganapati, a brother of Jagadhara, had installed the image of Dani Vinayaka.[81] Thus, this inscription gives important information regarding the image of Dani Vinayaka, which is also significant from the point of view of iconographic study. Thus, the geographical factor provides us the use of rockstone for carving the images of deities. Inscriptions from Ajaigarh fort give us valuable information regarding the construction of temples in the fort by the high officials of Kayastha family. The present inscription from Ajaigarh is preserved in the Asiatic Society Museum at Kolkata. Its object is to record the establishment of a temple dedicated to Kesava at Jayapuradurga by

Nana, a minister of King Bhojavarman.[82] This inscription is also significant for the study of Vishnu's different incarnations. The surname Srivastva was earned for the first time by Haruka, an early member of the Kayastha family. The inscription also adds that some of ancestors of Nana were the ministers of Chandella kings. The inscription gives us the name of the poet Amara who had composed the *prasasti* and of its writer Pamsuhu, the son of Ayo, who held the charge of the *pratoli* of Jayapura fort.[83] The *Visnudharmottara Purana* refers to the installation of consecrated images in the forts.[84] The instruction was followed by the Chandella kings.

Another inscription from Ajaigarh fort is inscribed on the front face of the rock forming the roof of two small reservoirs of water, locally known as Ganga and Yamuna. This inscription begins with a verse in praise of the river goddess Ganga. It traces the origin of the Chandella dynasty from the Moon and refers to the names of the rulers of the dynasty from Kirtivarman to Viravarman.[85] The object of the inscription is to record the construction of *Nirjara-Kupa* and *Prapa* at Ajaigarh and of a tank and hall at Nandipura by Viravarman's queen, Kalyanadevi. This inscription was composed by Ratampala, son of poet Haripala and grandson of poet Vatsraja, and engraved by the astisan Rama.[86] It gives us information regarding the work of public utility by a Chandella queen. This inscription also gives another name of Jayapusa as Nandipura.[87]

The Ajaigarh stone inscription of Abhaydeva is inscribed on the wall of a temple. It records the 'adoration to Isvara' by Abhayadeva, the son of *Asva-vaidya*, Thakura Bhojaka. The reference of *Asva-vaidya* is significant, that during the Chandella period there was provision for the treatment of horses.[88] This also refers to the existence of cavalry in the fort. This is associated with the geographical factor of the region. The Ajaigarh Santinatha image inscription is inscribed on the pedestal of a colossal image of Santinatha placed in a ruined Jain temple. This inscription records the installation of the image by Sadhu Sodhala, resident of Jayapuradurga during the time of Chandella king Viravarman, in AD 1279.[89] This inscription informs us regarding the prevalence of Jainism during the Chandella period and construction of a Jain temple and installation of the image of Santinatha. Another inscription discovered in the same temple gives us information regarding the installation of a Jain image by Acharaya Kumuda Chandra in the year 1274.[90] The inscription also mentions Muni Kunda, Kunda Acharya, Ghana Kirti and Mula Samgha.[91] Thus, this inscription provides much significant information regarding Jain sect at Ajaigarh fort. Ajaigarh inscription of Subhat is a well-preserved epigraph inscribed on a rock near the Tarhauni Gate of the fort. Its object is to record the construction of a temple by Subhata, a Vastavya Kayastha who held the post of the superindent of treasury during the reign of Chandella king Bhojavarman.[92] The epigraph gives information about Bhilas, Sabaras, and Pulindas who were defeated by Ananda, the Governor of the fort. Subhata and his wife Devaladevi are mentioned in other inscriptions also found in Ajaigarh and Panna.[93] On the rock at the Tarhoni Gate of Ajaigarh fort is a row of eight goddesses (the Ashtosakti), of whom seven are sitting and one standing. Their names are written below them.[94] Near these there is a cow and calf, and a four-armed goddess sitting with a child in lap, and with five pigs in pairs one above another on her left hand. This is evidently the figure of Shashti, the goddess of fecundity.[95] Ajaigarh fort is also considered a pilgrimage centre like Kalanjara as proved by these inscriptions.[96] Epigraphs and antiquities of Ajaigarh fort are important for the study of art and architecture. At Ajaigarh fort, we find both types of architecture, rock-cut and structural, due to the geographical setting of the fort. Similarly, we find epigraphic reference to various works of public utility as well as religious significance. We find the images of various deties belonging to Saiva, Vaisnava, Sakta and Jain cults. Thus, geographical environment of Ajaigarh also contributed a lot to the development of Chandella art and architecture. The fort of Ajaigarh was also a seat of civil administration of the Chandellas.[97] This fort town became a capital of the Chandellas in the later period of the dynasty. Thus, Chandella forts were occupied by kings, queens, ministers, civil and military officials, soldiers and merchants. It was also a centre of religious, commercial, art and literary activities as referred to in different inscriptions.

MAHOBA

The geographical and environmental setting of Mahoba played a significant role in shaping the town as the traditional capital of Chandellas. It lies at a distance of 140 km from Jhansi, about 80 km to Hamirpur and 65 km to the north of Khajuraho. Mahoba is a historical town of the Chandellas. The Chandellas, who were great warriors and builders, left behind an extraordinary legacy here. The impregnable fort on the hill played an important role in the traditional history of the Chandellas. The city of Mahoba can be called the pleasure city of the Chandellas. Its name is contraction of Mahotsavanagar or the city of festival, which was celebrated by Chandravarman, the traditional founder of Chandella dynasty.[98]

The Chandella kingdom is universally said to have been founded by Chandravarma, the son of Chandrama and the princess Hemavati, the daughter of the Gahirawars Raja of Benares or of his Purohit Hem Raj. God is believed to have informed the princess that her son would be born on the bank of the Karnavati or Kiyan River, the present Ken, and directed her to take him to Khajurahio, to offer him as a gift and to perform the sacrifice of a *Banda Jag*, to take away the reproach of her having become a mother without marriage.[99] Chandraverma is said to have built eighty-five temples[100] and founded the fort of Kalanjara. He then went to Mahoba, the place of Chandrama's 'great festival' *Mahotsava*, and made it his capital.[101] The Mahoba stone inscription is now preserved in the State Museum, Lucknow. Though very much mutilated, it gives very important information about the rulers of the Chandella dynasty. It traces its origin to the Moon, and seems to have mentioned all the rulers from Nannuka to Kirtivarman. About achievements, we are told that Jeja (Jayasakti) gave his name to Jejakabhukti. Dhanga equalled the powerful Hamvira (Subaktigin or Mahmud), Vidyadhara caused the destruction of the king of Kanyakubja and was worshipped by King Bhojadeva (Paramara) and the king of the Kalachuris, Vijayapala curbed the pride of Gangeyadeva (Kalachuri) and Kirtivarman defeated Laksmikarna. The rest of the inscription is lost. Thus, this inscription gives valuable information regarding Chandella rulers and their achievements.[102]

Cunningham discovered several short inscriptions on the pedestals of broken Jain images. Some of these are valuable, as they give both the date and the name of the reigning king at the time when the image was set up. Some omit the king's name, but record the date, whilst others omit both.[103]

The earliest of these short records from Mahoba contain only few words or only date; it most probably belongs to the time of Jayavarman Deva.[104] A second fragment, dated in Samvat 1203, gives the name of the sculptor Lakhana. A third inscription on the pedestal of a figure with shell symbol consists of two lines, which gives the name of Neminatha and Rupakara Lakhana. A fourth inscription with goose symbol (Sumatinatha), gives only the date.[105] A fifth inscription with the elephant symbol (Ajitnath) gives the date and name of the worshipper. A sixth inscription gives the name of the above worshipper together with those of his wife and four sons. A seventh incomplete inscription belongs to the reign of Paramardideva.[106] These seven short inscriptions give valuable information regarding the popularity of Jainism in Mahoba region as also regarding the ruling kings.

Pl. 1. Lakshman Temple, Khajuraho.

Pl. 2. *Yajna Varaha*, Khajuraho.

Pl. 3. Visvanatha Temple, Khajuraho.

Pl. 4. Devi Jagadambi Temple, Khajuraho.

Pl. 5. Kandariya Mahadeva temple, Khajuraho.

Pl. 6. *Anga Sikhars* of Temple, Khajuraho.

Pl. 7. *Mandapa* of Nilakantha Temple, Kalanjara.

Pl. 8. *Mukha Linga*, Siva Nilakantha, Kalanjara.

Pl. 9. Surroundings of Nilakantha Temple, Kalanjara.

Pl. 10. Sunset, Nilakantha Temple, Kalanjara.

Pl. 11. *Mandapa* of ruined temple, Ajaigarh.

Pl. 12. Ruined temples of Ajaigarh.

Pl. 13. *Dani* or *Vani Vinayaka*, Ajaigarh (Rock Art).

Pl. 15. Bodhisattva Simhanada Avalokitesvara, Mahoba.

Pl. 14. Sun Temple, Mahoba.

Pl. 16. Gate of Kalanjara Fort, Kalanjara.

The Mahoba copper-plate inscription of Paramardideva records the gift made on the occasion of *Makara Samkranti* by Paramardideva to Brahmana Ratan Sarman.[107] This copper-plate inscription gives us valuable information regarding the land donation on the occasion of *Makara Samkranti*. Among the monuments of Mahoba, Kakramatha occupies a rock island in the north-western corner of the Madan Sagar. It is a Saiva temple. Mahoba was also a subsidiary place of Manyadevi, the family deity of the Chandellas.[108] Mahoba was also a centre of Buddhism. Cunningham discovered the beautiful images of Buddha, Simhanand Lokesvara, Padmapani Avalokitesvara and Tara.[109] Thus, Mahoba was the centre of different religious cults.

Mahoba is famous for its tanks and lakes. The Chandella kings Rahil, Kirtivarman and Madanavarman constructed a large number of tanks associated with their names. These series of lakes created by them are brilliant engineering feats and their successful water management systems are still to be seen today. Mahoba was the centre of art and culture during the time of the Chandellas. This is due to its geographical environment.

KHAJURAHO

The famous town of Khajuraho, situated in Chhatarpur district of Madhya Pradesh, preserves the finest group of Hindu temples now existing in northern India.[110] Abu Rihan, who accompanied Sultan Mahmud in his campaign against Kalanjara in AD 1022, mentions it as Khajurahah, the capital of Jajahuti.[111] Ibn Batuta, who visited it about AD 1335, calls it Kajura and describes it having a lake about one mile in length surrounded by idol temples.[112] In a Chandella inscription we find the term Kharjjura-Vahaka, which is the older name of Khajuraho.[113] There are no traces of fortifications at Khajuraho, but it is a walled town as the people refer the name to a pair of gold *Khajur* trees (date-palms) which, they say, were fixed on one of the city gates. A more natural derivation would have been from the *Khajur* tree amongst which the town was originally situated. At present, however, there are not many of these trees in the neighbourhood.[114]

Khajuraho preserves the country's largest and most significant groups of medieval temples. It is situated on the bank of Khudar Nala, a tributary of the Ken River. The region is surrounded by scenic, beautiful waterfalls, and the low-lying hills of the Vindhyan range, locally called Datla and Lavania Pahads, which create a lovely backdrop to the temple complex. Khajuraho is located in the picturesque surroundings of forest and historical monuments. There are a few interesting spots on the banks of the river Ken which rises from the Vindhyan hills, flows in a northerly direction and joins the Yamuna River.

The geographical and environmental backdrop of Khajuraho is very charming. It is closely located near the Panna National Park, in which are preserved many species of wild and endangered plants and animals. Forests, mostly those of teak-covered hilly areas, and the topography meadows valleys and grassy plateaus provide an excellent scenic beauty.

The geographical and environmental setting in Khajuraho is rural and the town is still surrounded by some beautiful teak forests of Chhatarpur and Panna districts. The region is free from major industries and is covered by forests. The environment and flora and funna are comparatively less disturbed.[115]

Man since his evolution on the earth could not detach himself from the broad influences exerted on him by the environmental geography. Nature broadly assisted him in living a much more comfortable and healthy life. The ancient Indian artists were using trees, plants and flowers as decorative motifs. One can see many wild species of trees, such as *amaltas*, *bahera*, *pankar, gular, mahua, siris* and *shisham* blooming on road-sides. Some common roadside exotics recently introduced in the area are the tree species of eucalyptus, prosopis, specigera, etc. The plants traditionally fancied for roadsides, which still remain, are *aam, jamun, neem, peepal, bar* and *shisham*.

The countryside of Khajuraho has typical flora and fauna different from the surrounding forests, for example tree species such as *neem, peepal, babul, ber, bargod, khejri, khajura,* etc. grow only in the countryside. These species do not occur inside the environment where they have birds responsible for their dispersal. The common countryside bird *Desi myana,* along with two other jungle *myanas*, *Bamni myana* and *Ablaki myana,* are the most important species doing long-distance dispersal of seeds, which they transport and deposit through their faeces. Besides *myanas*, some crows also serve for dispersal. There are two species of crows, *Desi kaua* and *Jangli kaua*. Commonly these two species seem to exclude each other and only rarely meet together, yet in Khajuraho both these species can be seen. Among the parrots, its *jungli* counterpart which is very rare, is *Hiraman tota*.[116]

Langurs and *banders* are common countryside species of monkeys. Although the former is a *jungli* species, the two species occur together and are commonly seen on village trees.

Some other countryside common mammals like foxes, hares and mangoose are frequently seen in and around the region. While moving around Khajuraho, one would frequently come across a large bird often moving in pairs, the *mokha*. The most beautiful bird which may be seen in the countryside of Khajuraho is the peacock. The male of this species makes beautiful dancing movement during the breeding season. The coming of spring invites *koels* to the scene, which is advertised by the crescendo of their love songs throughout the breeding season.

Another common bird, which is considered auspicious by the local people, is *neelkantha*. This bird could be seen along with *patriniga* sitting on telephone wires from where they take flight to catch flies and bees. Among the passerines, *baya* is perhaps the most interesting bird to attract attention. The nest of this bird is an engineering marvel. The bird nests on trees near water sources and streams. Among the grain-feeding birds, perhaps the most common are babblers, the *Sat bhais*.

The most common sunbird, which may be seen frequenting flowers, is *phul chuhi*. Another little bird which may be commonly seen hopping restlessly among flowers and foliage is *phul sungni,* which is supposed to be responsible for the distribution and dispersal of parasitic plants Loranthus and Viscum, locally known as 'Banda'. The beginning of the spring season invites a large number of birds to flowers and fruits; some important fruits and flowers eaten are *mahua, achar, kusum, peepal, bargad, ber* and *mokor*.

Teak forests of Panna and Chhatarpur surround Khajuraho. Although the structure of these forests changed a great deal during the past decade, they still retain their natural character. The dominant tree is *sagon* which is a corrupted name of the original Sanskrit word, 'Shak-van'. In fact, the Central Indian forests of ancient India were dominated by *Shakor shal*. The former species is so named after its large-sized leaves and latter species for its poles which were used for the construction of beams in the houses. Hence the name 'Shala'.

There are three main flowering seasons. Spring is end of the winter. Most birds pollinate trees and shrub species flower during the reason. These include species like *palash, mandar, barna, semal,* and *dhai*. The bird which visits such flowers are crows, *mynas*, *bulbuls*, sunbirds, etc. Some other trees which flower during spring are *kachnar, galgal, achar,* etc.

Summer and rain flowering trees have a strong component of butterfly and mothe-pollinated species. These species include *kadamba, kaikain, babul, khair, khejera, siris,* etc.[117]

Rain flowering trees and climbers have a characteristic component of fly and beetle flowers. *Sitaphal* and *kari* are typical pollinated trees.

Although autumn is a season when grassy plains and hills are covered with a large number of flowering herbs and climbers, some important tree species also bloom during this season.

This present study of environmental backdrop shows that Khajuraho and its surroundings have a thick forest area.

The ancient literature, *Ramayana* of Valmiki, mentions this region as Vindhyatavi which is full of dense forests. Jejakabhukti was extremely rich in forest resources. Useful timber trees, fruit trees and medicinal trees were in abundance. The rich forests and the plentiful rains had rendered this region rich and supportive of humans as well as of wildlife. The wildlife in this tract has been so rich that during the times of Chandella rule, the forests around Khajuraho were used for hunting the wild animals as reflected in several Khajuraho sculptures.[118] Similarly, we find depiction of lions and elephants in large number showing their presence in the forests around Khajuraho had been so rich that at the time of Moghul rule at Delhi, the forests around Panna were used for hunting elephants. Like the vegetational diversity, the wildlife here also was quite diverse and rich. Tiger, panther, leopard, wild boar, bear, antelopes of several types, *nilgai,* ravine deer, spotted deer, *sambhar,* fox and jackals, etc. were found all over the forests which surround Khajuraho. The rivers, particularly Ken and Dhasan, used to be full of crocodiles. We find reflection of crocodiles in the *makara-torana*s of Khajuraho temples.[120] Similarly, we find depiction of Ganga on crocodiles at the doors of the temples sanctum.[121]

There are some interesting places on the banks of the Ken River, which rises from the Vindhyan hills, flows in north direction and meets the Yamuna River. The river Ken used to be full of crocodiles. There is Ken Gharial sanctuary situated at the confluence of the Ken and Khudar Rivers at distance of 24 km from Khajuraho.

Hindu temple *sikhara,* however, is an ancient term of Indian architecture; it is used frequently both in the *Ramayana* and in the *Mahabharata,* when alluding to the *prasada* in the shape of a mountain, like Kailasha or Meru[122] with its storeys it is itself like a mountain,[123] whatever its actual form might have been, of which there is no clear indication given in the Epics. The *prasada*-high and dazzling like Mount Kailash in the Himalayas and like Mount Meru which is known only by mind, is the seat of divinity and the world mountain, symbol of the polar axis, the vertical which leads from the centre to the highest point. While the whole temple is generally likened to the mountain, the term *sikhara* in early *Vastu-shastra* generally applies to every variation of the superstructure, which rises from the perpendicular walls of the *prasada,* and covers its *garbhagrha.*

Lakshman is one of the most beautiful and well-planned temples of Khajuraho. The temple inscription[124] at present fixed in the porch states that King Yasovarman built this magnificent temple to install the Vaikuntha image that he acquired from his overlord, the Pratihara king, who in turn had received it from the ruler of Chamba region. The temple was consecrated by his son Dhangadeva in AD 959. Verse 42 of this famous Chandella inscription reads:

> he erected this charming splendid home of (Visnu) the enemy of Daityas which reveals the peaks of the mountain of snow: the gold Kalasa (pinnacle) of which illuminates the sky, (and) the banners of which fixed on high poles, swing the groups of the clouds to and fro, at sight of which the inhabitants of heaven, met together on festivals, filled with increasing delight are struck with wonder.[125]

In this inscription we find that the *sikhara* is compared with a snow mountain. The Khajuraho inscription of Kokkalla mentions that he caused to be erected a temple like the spotless great peaks of the mountain of snow, the lofty golden dome of which, because it is in contact with the fierce splendour of the Sun, became a spotless canopy for the glorious Lord

Vaidyanatha.[126] This temple was recently excavated by the Archaeological Survey of India.[127] The Khajuraho Visvanatha temple inscription, V.S. 1059, is now built in the wall of the entrance porch of Visvanatha temple. The object of the inscription is to record the construction of the temple of Sambhu by Dhanga. He erected this unanimously praised temple of Lord Sambhu, the chief of the gods, with its summit white like the autumnal clouds, while his chariot glided past the clouds embracing the golden Kalasa of the temple, Aruna the charioteer of the Sun, speckled with colour, regarded even the crest of Meru as lesser in height.[128] Inscriptional sources give information about Kridagiri and Kelisarasi (swimming ports).[129] Kridagiri resounded with the sweet notes of his 'Excellencies' sung by the Kirata women seated on spotless lotuses (and) on which groups of peacocks are made to dance by the bubbling noise of waterfall rushing down from its top.[130] Khajuraho inscription dated V.S. 1011 (AD 954) states that at the conquest of regions, his soldiers somehow managed to ascend the slopes of the snowy mountain, where plentiful flowers had been gathered by Uma from every tree of paradise, where the troops of horses became unmanageable with fright at the gurgling sound of the torrents of the Ganges (and) which were crowded with (his) mighty elephants, terrified at the rousing of lions suddenly awakened from their sleep.[131] The Khajuraho inscription of Kokkalla refers to the matchless town of Padmavati, decorated with lofty palaces, shining white high-topped walls and palatial dwellings.[132] Kokkalla caused to be built a wonderful town which was furnished with big arches of great value and with dwellings 'highly decorated, lofty shining great gates, resembling the city of Indra'.[133] Inscriptions refer to lakes and tanks full of water in which the lotuses shine with loveliness of the spreading rays of the bright-lustred moon.[134] The Khajuraho stone inscription of Yasovarman refers to the halls of princes, where sages dwell, (and) where good people meet, in the village, in the assemblages of the lowly, among the rows of shop merchants, (and) where streets cross, where wanderers talk together on the road, (and) in the huts of the dwellers of the forests, everywhere everybody, constantly from astonishment, is loud only in praise of his excellencies.[135] This inscriptional reference gives us a graphic description of urban and rural life during the time of the Chandellas. The Khajuraho stone inscription of Dhangadeva of V.S. 1059 (AD 1002) refers to the construction of a lake, 'Bivarnava', larger than the sea and he also erected a unanimously praised temple of Vaikuntha, the enemy of the Titans, from which (temple) the charioteer of the sun turned away the chariot to save the wheels because with its sharp spires shining like the autumnal moon it pierces the planets and its golden Kalasa is mistaken for the sun kissing with its orb the peaks of the snowy mountains.[136] The Ajaigarh stone inscription of Kirtivarman also refers to the mountain Kailasha.[137] An inscription of Khajuraho informs us that Dhanga had exacted a magnificent temple and its *torana* was a creation of Visvakarma himself, who had entered into the body of the architect.[138] Khajuraho Jinanatha temple inscription, V.S. 1011 (AD 954), records the gift of seven gardens by Pahilla, who was honoured by King Dhanga, probably of the same temple.[139] The following are the names of the gifted gardens.

(1) Pahilla garden
(2) Chandra garden
(3) Little Chandra garden
(4) Sankara garden
(5) Pancha Itala-Vatika
(6) Mango garden
(7) Dhanga garden house.[140]

The Khajuraho inscription of Dhanga of V.S. 1059 (AD 1002) states: "As long as earth with its mountains, cities and trees is enclosed by the oceans, as long as the sun shines and the moon oozes out nectar, as long as this globe of universe lasts and the immobile are fixed; so long may this royal temple, making Mount Kailasha, continue."[141] This passage of the inscription gives information regarding the various aspects of natural forces.

The geographical environment around Khajuraho is a fairly picturesque upland, well covered with trees and shrubs and watered by rivers and tanks. Geologically, the region forms the part of Bundelkhand gneiss outcrop, bounded on the south by the Ken, and its tributaries which have cut deep gorges through the massive Vindhyan sandstones.[142] The upper Vindhyan or Kaimur sandstones provide excellent building material in the form of a fine grained sandstone of rich shade varying from pale buff to light red, which has been largely used for the Khajuraho temples.[143] The history of the Chandellas cannot be completed without the study of the Khajuraho temples. All the important standing temples at Khajuraho are in a fairly good condition and their preservation is mainly due to the geographical position of Khajuraho, which did not come in the way of Muslim iconoclasts.[144] Khajuraho is located in the beautiful scenic surroundings of mountains, rivers, waterfalls, forests and historical monuments.

NOTES AND REFERENCES

1. Gale, *Environmental Encylopedia* (2nd Edition), Introduction, p. xxi.
2. *Ibid.*
3. R.K. Dikshit, *Chandellas of Jejakabhukti*, p. 11.
4. *Ramayana* (Gita Press), 11, 94.
5. R.K. Dikshit, *op. cit.*, p. 12.
6. Ajay Mitra Shashti, *Varahamihra's India*, Vol. II, p. 395.
7. *Ibid.*
8. Stella Kramrisch, *The Hindu Temple*, Vol. I, p. 4.
9. *Ibid.*
10. *Ibid.*
11. *Ibid.*, p. 5.
12. *Ibid.*
13. *Ibid.*
14. Urmila Agrawal, *Khajuraho Sculptures and their Significance*, p. 5.
15. Bhoja, *Samarangana Sutradhara*, Chap. 34, 30-31.
16. Tasapada Bhattacharya, *The Canons of Indian Art*, p. 282.
17. A. Cunnigham, *A.S.I.R.*, Vol. XXI, p. 20.
18. *Vaman Purana*, India, 90/27, *Epigraphia Indica*, Vol. 1, pp. 127-28; *Epigraphia Indica*, Vol. XXX, pp. 87-90.
19. A. Cunnigham, *op. cit.*, Vol. XXI, p. 22.
20. *Mahabharata* (Pune Edn.), 3/83/53; 3/85/13-15, 13/26/33; *Valmiki Ramayana*, 7/2/39. *Vayu Purana*, 23/104, *Padma Purana*, 81/18-38/15, *Skanda Purana*, 14/6/25, *Garuda Purana*, 81/18/19, *Brahma Purana*, 2/146/1, *Matsya Purana* 32/109, *Brahmand Purana*, 3/13/100.
21. A. Cunningham, *op. cit.*, Vol. XXI, p. 22.
22. *Ibid.*
23. *Mahabharata*, 3/83/53; 3/85/13-15, 13/26/33, *Valmiki, Ramayana*, 7/2/39.
24. *Vayu Purana*, 23/104, *Padma Purana*, 81/18, 38/15, *Agni Purana* 32/108, *Matsya Purana*, 32/109.
25. B.N. Roy (ed.), *Kalanjara: A Historical and Cultural Profile*, p. 2.
26. S.K. Sullerey, *Ajaigarh Aur Kalanjara Ki Devapratimayain*, pp. 23-24.
27. *Epigraphic India*, Vol. XXXI, p. 162, *A.S.I.A.R.*, 1935-36, p.93.
28. *Ibid.*
29. S.K. Sullerey, *op. cit.*, pp. 78-88.
30. *Ibid.*, pp. 15-16.
31. A. Cunningham, *op. cit.*, Vol. XXI, pp. 21-22.
32. S.K. Sullerey, *op. cit.*, pp. 78-88.

33. A. Cunningham, *op. cit.*, Vol. XXI, p. 20.
34. H.C. Ray, *Dynastic History of India*, Vol. II, p. 693, Muslim Chroniclers mention the strength of his army as follows:
    1. Nizam-ud-din- 36000 horses, 1,45000 foot, 350 (Var 640) elephants (T.A. (D), p.12.
    2. Ibn-ul. Athir- 56,000 horses, 184000 foot, 746 elephants (D.N.H.1), II -p. 690, n. 2.
    3. Gardizi- 36,000 horses, 1,45000 foot, 640 elephants (K.Z.A. p.76).
    4. Frishta- 36,000 horses, 45,000 foot, 640 elephants (T.F.(B)) 1, p. 64.
    5. Farukhi-36,000 horses, 1,33000 foot, 900 elephants (Vide L.T.S.M.G, p. 112, n. 1).
35. A. Cunningham, *op. cit.*, Vol. II XXI, p. 23.
36. Nitisara Kamandak, XIV. 29.
37. *Ibid.*, IV. 59.
38. *Ibid.*, X. 56.
39. *Ibid.*, XIV, 28-30.
40. Kautilya, *Arthasastra*, Vol. 11, 3, 4.
41. *Epigraphia Indica*, Vol. 1, p. 327
42. *Indian Antiquary*, Vol. XVIII, pp. 235-39.
43. *Ibid.*, Vol. XXXVII, p. 132.
44. N.S. Bose, *op. cit.*, p. 11.
45. R.S. Sharma, *Indian Feudalism*, pp. 237-41.
46. S.K. Mitra, *Early Ruler of Khajuraho*, pp.163-64.
47. S.K. Sullerey, *op. cit.*, p. 724.
48. Prof. V.S. Pathak suggested the reading after seeing this inscription of Pandu Varmsi Udyan.
49. *Suktimuktavali*, p. 46.
50. *Epigraphia Indica*, Vol. VII, pp. 85-93.
51. *Ibid.*
52. *Ibid.*, Vol. XIX, p. 18.
53. *Ibid.*
54. N.S. Bose, *op. cit.*, p. 2.
55. *Epigraphia Indica*, Vol. 1, pp. 127-28.
56. N.S. Bose, *op. cit.*, p. 44.
57. R.C. Majumdar, *Ancient India*, p. 351.
58. S.K. Sullerey, *op. cit.*, p. 63.
59. Briggs Farishta, Past I, p. 18.
60. A. Cunningham, *op. cit.*, Vol. XXI, p. 34.
61. *Epigraphia Indica*, Vol. VII, pp. 85-93.
62. N.S. Bose, *op. cit.*, p. 44.
63. Briggs Farishta, Part I, p.18.
64. S.K. Sullerey, *Ajaigarh aur Kalanjasa ki Devapratimayain*, p. 18.
65. H.C. Roy, *D.H.N.I.*, Vol. II, p. 683.
66. A. Cunningham, *op. cit.*, Vol. XXI, p. 29.
67. Prof. V.S. Pathak's reading of the inscription.
68. S.D. Trivedi, *Bundelkhand Ka Puratattava*, pp. 10-11.
69. S.K. Sullerey, *op. cit.*, p. 24.
70. A. Cunningham, *op. cit.*, Vol. XXI, p. 46.
71. *Ibid.*
72. *Epigraphia Indica*, Vol. I, pp. 325-330.
73. *Indian Antiquary*, XXXVII, p. 135.
74. N.S. Bose, *op. cit.*, p. 134.
75. *Ibid.*
76. *Epigraphia Indica*, VoI. XXX. p. 87.
77. A. Cunningham, *op. cit.*, Vol. XXI, p. 49.
78. *Ibid.*, pp. 49-50.

79. *Ibid.*
80. *Epigraphia Indica,* Vol. XXX, pp. 87-90.
81. N.P. Chakravarti, *A.S.I.R.*- 1335-36, p. 91.
82. *Epigraphia Indica,* Vol. XXVIII, pp. 98-107.
83. *Ibid.*
84. Urmila Agrawal, *Significance of Khajuraho Sculptures,* p. 5, n. 2.
85. *Epigraphia Indica,* Vol. I, pp. 323-330.
86. *Ibid.*
87. *Ibid.*
88. A. Cunningham, *op. cit.,* XXI, p. 51.
89. N.P. Chakravarti, *op. cit.,* pp. 91-92.
90. R.K. Dikshit, *op. cit.,* pp. 207-08.
91. *Ibid.*
92. *Epigraphia Indica,* Vol. 1, pp. 330-338.
93. R.K. Dikshit, *op. cit.,* pp. 210-11.
94. A. Cunningham, *op. cit.,* Vol. XXI, p. 53.
95. *Ibid.,* p. 47.
96. A. Cunningham, *op. cit.,* Vol. XXI, p.51.
97. N.S. Bose, *op. cit.,* p. 135.
98. *Ibid.,* p. 13.
99. A. Cunningham, *op. cit.,* Vol. XXI, p. 70.
100. *Ibid.,* p. 70, fn. 2 .
101. *Ibid.*
102. *Epigraphia Indica,* Vol. I, pp. 217-222.
103. A. Cunningham, *op. cit.,* Vol. XXI, p. 73.
104. *Ibid.*
105. *Ibid.*
106. *Ibid.*
107. *Epigraphia Indica,* Vol. XVI, pp. 9-15.
108. A.P. Pandey, *Chandella Kalin Bundelkhand,* p. 96.
109. N.S. Bose, *op. cit.,* p. 170.
110. A. Cunningham, *op. cit.,* Vol. XXI, p. 55, fn. 1.
111. *Ibid.*
112. *Ibid.,* p. 56.
113. *Epigraphia Indica,* Vol. I, pp. 137-147.
114. A. Cunningham, *op. cit.,* Vol. XXI, p. 55.
115. T.C. Mojupuris and Indra, *Glories of Khajuraho,* p. 261.
116. *Ibid.,* p. 262.
117. *Ibid.,* pp. 264-65.
118. Krishna Deva, *Temples of Khajuraho,* Vol. I, pp. 278-79.
119. *Ibid.,* pp. 279-80.
120. *Ibid.,* p. 44.
121. *Ibid.,* p. 49.
122. Stella Kramrisch, *op. cit.,* Vol. I, p. 182.
123. *Ibid.*
124. *Epigraphia Indica,* Vol. I, 121 f.
125. *Ibid.,* pp. 122-135.
126. *Ibid.,* pp. 147-152.
127. Devangana Desai, *Khajuraho,* pp. 76-78.
128. *Epigraphia Indica,* Vol. I, pp. 137-47.
129. *Ibid.,* pp. 122-35.
130. *Ibid.*

131. *Epigraphia Indica*, Vol. I, pp. 122-135.
132. *Ibid.*, Vol. I, pp. 147-152.
133. *Ibid.*
134. *Ibid.*
135. *Ibid.*, pp. 122-135.
136. *Ibid.*, pp. 137-147.
137. *Ibid.*, Vol. XXX, pp. 87-90.
138. *Ibid.*, Vol. I, pp. 137-147.
139. *Ibid.*, Vol. I, pp. 135-136.
140. *Ibid.*
141. *Ibid.*
142. *Ibid.*, Vol. I, pp. 137-147.
143. Krishna Deva, *The Temples of Khujuraho*, Vol. I, p.
144. N.S. Bose, *op. cit.*, p. 162.

4

Forestry and Wildlife

Man, since his evolution on the earth, could not detach himself from the broader influence exerted on him by the environmental elements. Nature broadly assisted him in living a much more comfortable and healthy life. It was only from his surroundings that he got food to eat, medicines to counter the baneful effects of diseases, and shelter from inclement weather and, last but not the least, fuel to warm himself and also to cook food for its better relish.[1] In fact, the forest played a great role in the economic life of the people. They depended upon it not only for their fuel and food, but also for their clothes.

It is generally accepted that the region over which Chandellas ruled was full of thickly grown forests towards the beginning of the pre-historic period. It was situated within the monsoon belt and had good rainfall and fertile soil favourable to wild growth of various kinds of trees, plants and shrubs. Many rivers flowing in different parts of the region helped further in their growth. The segment of Jejakabhukti has been witness to historical and cultural process right from the pre-historic periods. The Lower Palaeolithic has been reported from Belharka on the Ken River (near Naraini, Banda district), Ramchandra hill (near Naraini) and a few other sites. The discovery of an Achulean factory in the region is of great importance for tracing the processes of tool-making. Siddhapur (Karwi) has given us middle and upper Palaeolithic examples. Near Kalanjara, an upper Palaeolithic factory site has been discovered. The stone tools of Anchivara and Lodhawara are also worth notice. Neolithic and Microlithic tools have also been reported from Banda. Pre-historic cultures had developed in this region due to thick forests and river valleys, which provided them food and other amenities to live in this area. Cockburn was the first to discover rock-paintings in this region from Markundi and Maghagawan. Rock art has been reported from other places such as Sarhat, Malvan and Kuriyakunj. Amva, Bargarh and Uldan near Manikpur also give indication of the development of rock-art in this region. Many pre-historic rock-painting sites have been discovered from the Jejakabhukti region.[2] I have also discovered some rock-paintings in and around Kalanjara. The name of Chitrakuta evidently was derived from Chitra (painting) and Kuta (hill). Thus, Chitrakuta means a hill of paintings, which is why it even attracted the attention of Rama.[3]

Cunningham identified the cities and peoples of ancient India mentioned by Pliny and Ptolemy.

SANDRABATIS

This district is bound on the west by Kaspiraei, whose territory included Madura, or the holy city of Mathura of the present day. To the south lay the Vindhya mountains, and to the east the Tamasis, or Tons River. These landmarks make it easy to guess that the province of Sandrabatis derived its name from the Charmanavati, or Chambal River, that it comprised the whole of the country lying between the Chambal and Tons Rivers, thus including the northern half of the present Gwalior territory, with the whole of Bundelkhand and a strip of Rewa.[4] The towns of Sandrabatis mentioned by Ptolemy are: 1. Tamasis, 2. Kuraporina, 3. Empalathra, and 4. Nadubandagar. The first of these may be identified with the famous hill of Kalanjara, which, before it was fortified, was well known as the favourite abode of *tapaswis* or 'ascetics'. H.H. Wilson says it is mentioned in the Vedas, and that it was one of the *Tapasya-Sthanas* or 'spots adapted to practise of austere devotion'. By a very slight change the Greek *Tamasis* may be read as *tapasis*.[5] The name of Kalanjaradri, or the hill of Kalanjara, is said to have been derived from Siva himself, who as Kala, or 'Time', causes all things to decay (*jara*), and who is therefore destroyer of all things, and the god of death. *Tapaswis* or ascetics of Kalanjara were therefore devoted to the worship of Siva.[6] Thus, situated in the middle of Vindhyan forest, Kalanjara attracted the attention of ancient sages, who found this site very congenial for penance. Thus, during the Vedic period, Kalanjara gained a significance for performance and penance. The literary sources indicate that several ascetics had their *ashramas* in and around the Kalanjara. According to local tradition, the *ashramas* of such renownd saints as Valmiki, Vedavyasa, Atri and Agastya were located here.[7] These *ashramas* (hermitages) contributed to the progress of various facets of culture in and around the region.

During the time of the epics, Kalanjara transformed into a *tirthasthala*. *Mahabharata* refers to Kalanjara as a place of spiritual meditation.[8] In the same epic, Kalanjara is referred to as a place famous in the whole country.[9] It also refers to a 'Hiranya-vindu' on the Kalanjara mountain.[10] *Mahabharata* refers to a tank of gods on Kalanjara mountain.[11] The *Ramayana* also refers to Kalanjara as a religious centre.[11]

Forests are mentioned in the epics. The *Mahabharata* mentions many forests and mountains having innumerable trees, and describes the Daivavana, the Kauranchavana and others. It also describes the different trees grown in them.[12] The *Ramayana* too describes many forests, located in various parts of the country. It refers to forests called Matanga[13] and Dandkaranya. It appears that Rama lived for some time on Mount Chitrakuta during his exile. Thus, Chitrakuta has been included among the holy *tirthas* from the time of epics.

Forests had been recognised during the later Vedic period as economic resources for state. Deforestation was discouraged in the sixth century BC. The burning of forests on a large scale was no longer liked by the people in spite of the urbanisation in various parts of India during sixth century BC. Ashoka promulgated an edict that forests should not be burnt either uselessly or in order to destroy living beings.[14] The *Arthasastra* of Kautilya gives an account of forest and forest produce. He suggests the king to appoint superintendent of forest produce to collect timber and other products of forests by employing those who guard forests. Describing his duties Kautilya states further that "he shall not only start productive works in forests, but also fix adequate fines and compensation to be levied from those who cause any harm to productive forests except in calamities".[15] His other duty, as prescribed by Kautilya, was to carry on, either inside or outside the capital city, the manufacture of all kinds of articles which were necessary for life or for the defence of forts.

> The *Arthasastra* describes three kinds of forests, game forests and timber forests of two kinds. One was maintained for the sports of the king and the other which was open to the public. The game forest made for the king was, according to *Arthasastra,* an extensive forest, provided with only one entrance, rendered inaccessible by construction of ditches all around, with plantation of delicious fruit trees, bushes, bowers, and thornless trees, with an expansive lake of water, full of harmless animals and with tigers, beasts of prey, male and female elephants, young elephants and bisons – all deprived of their claws and teeth.

The game forest open to the public was made on the extreme limit of the country or in some other suitable locality. This too had different kinds of game beasts.

The third kind of forests, mentioned in the *Arthasastra,* were the elephant forests, which were preserved on the extreme limits of the country, spared from wild tracts.[16] In the time of Kautilya, such forests were situated in Kalinga, Anga and east Dasarna, from where different kinds of elephants were found. The *Arthasastra* of Kautilya suggests thorny plants and poisonous plants on the ramparts surrounding a fort.[17]

The region of Jejakabhukti played a significant role during the Mauryan period. The different epigraphs, viz., the Panguraria inscription, the Minor Rock Edicts of Rupanath (Jabalpur district of M.P.) and Gujarra (Datia district of M.P.) prove that this region of Jejakabhukti was included in the Mauryan empire. The Rupanath edict makes it very clear that the regions around Rupanath were included within Ashokan dominions. The Minor Rock Edict was issued while Ashoka was touring the area to meet his subjects. Thus, the entire region of Jejakabhukti was included in the Mauryan empire.

The Shahbazgarhi Rock Edict XIII of Ashoka mentions the name of Atavikas, a forest tribe. It seems that the Atavikas belonged to the forest region of Jejakabhukti. Thus we can conclude that this region had good forests during the Mauryan period. Ashoka ordered various trees for the benefit of the people and animals to be planted. Reference to this area is available in his inscriptions, one of which describes thus:

> Everywhere in the dominions of King Priyadarsi, beloved of the Gods, as well as of those of his frontier sovereigns such as Colas, Pandyas, Satiyaputra, Keralaputra, as far as Tamraparni, the Yona king called Amtiyoka – wherever medicinal herbs, wholesome for men and wholesome for animals, are not found, they have everywhere been caused to be imported and planted. Roots and fruits, wherever they are not found, have been caused to be imported and planted. In the road sides, wells have been caused to be dug and trees caused to be planted for the enjoyment of men and animals.[18]

He had trees planted for shade and mango-groves for fruits; he had banyan trees planted to give shade to men and animals, had groves of mango trees planted at every half-*kosa,* had wells dug; rest-houses had been erected and numerous watering places had been provided by him here and there for the enjoyment of men and beasts.[19] Ashoka constructed many hospitals where people were cured of their diseases. He mentions in one of his inscriptions that everywhere in his kingdom, he had established medical hospitals for treatment of men.[20] Ashoka also established hospitals for the treatment of animals in the dominion.[21] Thus, he made a great contribution in the field of forestry for the welfare of men and animals equally.

The art history of the region, in its true and proper perspective, starts from Sunga period. The art of the region, like that of any other part, reflects the socio-economic and religious traits in their changing context and people's behaviour. The unique environmental factors, forests, developed land, water resources and hilly ranges played a vital role in determining the mediums, forms and tradition of the indigenous art. The art of the region exhibits the common upsurge of the people at large, including kings, nobles, common men, priestly class, business community, and tribals living in the forests, ascetics living in the huts and peasantry, who strived hard and offered their best to lay down norms and develop early forms of Indian architecture and sculpture, which were first experimented in Madhyadesa and later transmitted to other regions.

The art of Bharhut was based on native traditions, which suited the socio-religious requirements of an agrarian society. It reflects the simple, unsophisticated and indigenous trends, the myths and plain story-telling technique. The *Jataka* stories are depicted in such a simple narrative method that the onlookers can understand and drive inspiration from them. The human figures, their dresses, ornaments, etc. are drawn from the living groups of people of the region. The background of sculptural panels are filled with indigenous plants, flowers, birds and animals. The entire artistic panorama moves as a devotee goes forward, enjoying the panels and identifying himself with the existing atmosphere. The popular faiths and concepts of an agrarian society, pertaining to Yakshas, Nagas, tree-spirits, Gandharavas and Vidyadharas are interwoven into the stories in such a fascinating manner that the people in general must have felt elevated to a higher plane, losing their identity. This unique identification of self with divine drama probably made the Bharhut art alive and brought it nearer to the people. The Bharhut reliefs depict traits, trends and customs of a pastoral society. Even the flora and fauna referred to in the *Jataka*s belong to this region. The male and female figures of reliefs are actual models selected from the living society. The artist might have taken note of the feminine beauty to depict the Yakshi and other divine dancing figures such as Sudarasana and Almbushra, etc.[22] Cunningham has rightly pointed out that the dresses and ornaments too are drawn from the Bharhut area and some of them are still in practice.[23] The Bharhut sculptor, who drew inspiration from living models of the pastoral society, has made a very faithful depiction of the typical tribal social customs, manners, dresses and ornaments. Bharhut sculptures represent the day to day life of the village folk in their natural habitat. The female figures of Bharhut railings exhibit even the tattoo marks (*godna*) carved on their faces and body, which is still a living tradition. Cunningham remarks,

> Now, it is a curious fact that not only are all the female in the Bharhut sculptures more or less ornamented with tattoo marks, but they are all dressed in the same short *dhoti*-petticoat of the present inhabitants. Their ornaments were of silver and gold and studded with precious and semi-precious stones as are used even to day.

The Bharhut sculptors were conscious of the rich and variegated flora and fauna of their region. This innate love of nature exuberates everywhere through the meticulously carved lotus flowers, stalks, garlands, creepers, plants and birds and animals which dominate the moving panorama of Bharhut art. Even the human figures, wherever carved, are shown as a part and parcel of this overflowing natural phenomenon. Thus, the art of Bharhut reflects the environment prevailing during the Sunga period. This also gave inspiration to the future Chandella artists.

According to the drama, *Malavikagnimitram* of Kalidas, Verasena, a collateral brother of the queen of Agnimitra, was appointed as a commander of a frontier fortress which stood on the banks of the river Mandakini.[25] Pargiter has shown only two rivers of this name, one in the Banda district of Uttar Pradesh, and the other in the south.[26] The river Mandakini of the play must be located in the Banda district, as the dominions of the Sungas did not extend beyond Narmada in the south. Further, the kingdom of Agnimitra extended around the upper part of Central India. Hence, the fortress on the bank of Mandakini, which was governed by a collateral brother of the queen of Agnimitra, must be placed somewhere within the dominions of Agnimitra only. We can venture to identify this fortress of Sungas with the forts of Kalanjara which lie not far from the river Mandakini.[27] According to Cunningham, whose view is based on the epigraphical and other archaeological sources, "the fortress may have been founded at least as early as the beginning of Christian era."[28] It is highly probable that the early Sungas, taking the geographical situation into consideration, constructed the fortress of Kalanjara to defend their southern frontiers.[29] Thus, the above description of sculptures of Bharhut gives the tribal and forest background of region. The sculpture art of Bharhut depicts the *Parnakuti* (hermitage made of leaves) of the ascetics, which also reflects the forest surroundings. Thus, the sculptural art of Bharhut reflects the forests surrounding of this region. It can be presumed on the basis of sculptural art that the region was covered with thick forests and tribal people lived in the region during the Sunga period. Most of the scholars believe that it was Samudra Gupta who brought the region of Bundelkhand and eastern Malwa under the direct sway of the imperial Guptas. An inscription from Eran (Sagar district, M.P.) of Samudra Gupta mentions that he made the city of Eran a resort of self-enjoyment (*Svabhogenagara*).[30] He also conquered Atavika territory, including the Dabhala region extending up to Jabalpur[31] also, the eighteen forest kingdoms referred to in the Khoh copper-plate inscription of Samkoha (G.E. 209-AD 529).[32] These kingdoms were apparently in Bundelkhand region and Dahala or the Jabalpur region.[33] Samksobha was a Parivrajaka Maharaja ruling over this part of Central India, a feudatory of the Guptas. Earlier, the forest kingdoms were conquered by the Gupta ruler.[34] It may be noted here that Allahabad *prasasti*, like the *Mahabharata*,[35] distinguishes the Atavikas from Kantaras, both referring to the forest region.[36] The term 'Vindhyatavi', the forests of the Vindhya mountain (which are so often referred to in one of the customary imprecatory verse used in inscriptions), is given by Monier William in his *Sanskrit Dictionary* as seeming to have denoted originally the whole extent of country from Mathura to the Narmada. It would be very suitably represented by general term 'forest countries' or forest kingdoms. A somewhat similar term 'Vanarashtra' forest countries and 'Vana rajaya' forest kingdom occurs in the *Brihat Samhita*.[37] But the countries there speak of India mapped by Varahamihira, and they are, at any rate, Maharaja Hastin.[38] Thus, we can precisely say that this region during the Gupta period was surrounded by forests and there were several forest kingdoms existing here and the region was full of forests. We get information from the Puranic literature related to the religious importance of Kalanjara as a famous *tirtha* of India. *Padma Purana* refers to Kalanjara as destroyer of great sins.[39] Similarly, *Garuda Purana* mentions that Kalanjara is capable of destroying all types of sins and giving liberation.[40] *Brahma Purana* also describes that Kalanjara can destroy all the sins.[41] In Puranic literature, we find mention of Kalanjara as Maha Tirtha,[42] Uttam Tirtha,[43] and Param Tirtha.[44] Kalanjara is also referred to as Brahma Kshetra[45] and Puroshotam Kshetra,[46] in the *Puranas*. In the *Padma Purana,* Kalanjara is described as Ukhala,[47] which exists in nine places in India. It is also described as the finest mountain in *Vayu*[48] and *Linga Puranas*.[49] In the *Padma Purana,* Kalanjara is described as a place of 'Atama Sadhana'.[50] Kalanjara is mentioned as 'Vana' (forest) in *Shivopnisad*.[51] Similarly, we can identify 'Tungakarayana'[52] and 'Tapasaranya[53] described in the *Mahabharata*. All these references of Puranic literature indicate that the region around Kalanjara was surrounded by very thick forests.

The early history of Harsha's region is reconstructed from a study of Banabhatta who was his court poet and who wrote the *Harsha Charita*. From the *Harsha Charita* we know that Harsha went to Vindhyatavi in search of his sister Rajyasri. He traced her in the Vindhyatavi. Thus, the reference of *Harsha Charita* shows that during the time of Harsha this region was considered as a forest of Vindhya mountain.

References to the development of forestry are available in the literary works of Kalidas, Bhairavi, and Magha. They give a vivid description of different seasons, creepers, blooming flowers and a large number of fruit trees adorned with flowers and fruits. During this period the offering of flowers too became the main item of worship of gods and goddesses, due to the growth of devotional worship.

> The Mandasura inscription of Kumaragupta and Bandhuvarman describes Dasapura in the following way: Here the lakes, crowned with Karandava ducks are beautiful having the water close to their shores made variegated with many flowers that fall from the trees growing on the banks and being adorned with water lilies in full bloom. The lakes are beautiful with the swans that are engaged in the pollen that falls from the water lilies shaken by the tremulous waves and in other places with the water-lillies bent down by the great burden of their filaments. Here the woods are adorned with lovely trees, that are bowed down by the weight of their flowers and are full of the sounds of the flights of bees that hum loudly through intoxication and with the women from the city who are perpetually singing.[54]

There are many references in the *Puranas* dealing with the importance of trees and conservation of groves and gardens. The *Agni Purana* states that the planting of the trees and the construction of pleasure-gardens are conducive to purgation of sin and enjoyment of prosperity. [55] It further recommends that,

> the man who plants trees bearing fruits and flowers for enjoyment of the public, attains a supreme state of bliss. The man who plants thirty trees, giving shade, fruits and flowers and ten mango trees, is not destined to go to hell. The man who plants trees, giving fragrant flowers and sweet fruits is re-born, as a result, as a Brahman in prosperous country; one should worship trees as one worships a sage free from the vice of envy, because it provides shade, and fruits and flowers even to its cutter. The all giving 'Tree-son' which does not bear a grudge even to its 'cutter-father' out of selfish consideration brings about the complete salvation to the planter. So, the Brahmanas should always plant them with due ceremony and treat them as their sons.[56]

Another reference similar to the above is found in the *Varaha Purana,* which states that "a man by planting trees, attains the same bliss as he does by the gift of cows and land, just as a pious son saves the family. Just as good but difficult rules, followed with care save fruits and save the planter." Thus, the plantation of trees was considered also a religious work.

The forestry acquires a clear focus during the Chandella period. The Jejakabhukti region was full of dense and thick forests. It was extremely rich in the resources of forests even up to the present times, which can be seen in the form of Panna National Park having useful timber trees, fruit trees and medicinal trees, which are in abundance. The rich forests and the plentiful rains had rendered this region rich and supportive of human beings as well as of wildlife.

References to the forestry are available in Chandella inscriptions. The Khajuraho inscription of AD 954 refers to forest fire thus:

> as the moon and the Kaustubha (arose) from the ocean of milk, so were born from home of wonder (Vakapati) two sons Jayasakti and Vijayasakti, when they are met together, enraptured praise with shaking of heads the deeds of both of them, by the unmeasured prowess of whom adversaries were destroyed as wood is burnt by a blazing fire.[57]

The same Khajuraho inscription refers to the tribal Kirata women in this way:

> Whose pleasure mount (was) that Vindhya, the peak of which are charming with sweet notes of his excellencies sung by Kirata women seated on spotless lotuses, (and) on which groups of peacocks are made to dance by the bubbling noise of waterfalls rushing down from the tops.[58]

This inscriptional reference gives a graphic description of forest environment as well as tribal women. Similarly, the same inscription gives a graphic description of the urban, rural and forest life of people during the Chandella period in this way:

> In the halls of princes, where sages dwell, (and) where good people meet, in the village, in the assemblages of the lowly, among the rows of shops of merchants, and where streets cross, where wanderers talk together on the road (and) in the huts of the dwellers of the forest, everywhere everybody constantly exclaims in astonishment only in praise of his excellencies.[59]

The Khajuraho inscription of Dhangadeva of the year AD 1002 refers to Kinnaras dwelling in caves. This is described in this manner: "By the Kinnaras (divine chorists), dwelling in caves, was song hand-in-hand with their comparisons, widely expanding their nostrils in exhilaration, melodious song of kings, bright fame."[60] The Ajaigarh inscription of the time of Bhojavarman states that one Ananda, born in the Vastavya Kyastha family of Jajuka, was appointed by Trailokyavarman as the Governor of the fort of Jayapura (Durgadhikasi). Ananda is credited for reducing to submission the wild tribes of Billas, Savaras and Pulindas.[61] Thus, Chandella inscriptions give us references regarding forests and forest and cave dwellers.

The Chandella inscription makes references to different types of plants. The Khajuraho inscription of AD 1002 refers to "obeisance to Rudra (who though) unborn (is) the cause of the high and huge holy banyan trees (who though) devoid of activities (is) the preserver and destroyer."[62] The Chandella inscription refers to Kalpavriksha (tree of Paradise) thus:

> Deep like the oceans, pleasing like the moon, radiant with the brilliance of the sun, firm like the earth, great like the noblest of mountains, munificent like the tree of paradise, till maturely, if anywhere there has been another lord charming with a multitude of spotless excellences, unchangeable to the end of world equal to Yasovarmani.[63]

The Khajuraho inscription of Kokkalla also refers to Kalpavriksha and also to excellent trees and creepers of good birth.[64] The Chandella inscriptions also mention mango trees and mango gardens. The Khajuraho Jinanatha temple inscription of AD 954 records the gift of the seven gardens by Pahila; one of them was a mango garden.[65] In the sculptural art of Khajuraho, we find depiction of mango fruits in the hands of deities. The Kalanjara stone inscription refers to Viravarman's work of public utility and pious benefactions. He is credited with the construction of various temples, gardens, ponds and tanks, and the installation of the image of Siva, Kamla and Kali in splendid homes.[66] The Augasi plates mention an ant-hill by a *maduka* tree as the western boundary of the gift land.[67] The trees of mango and *maduka* were referred to in Chandella inscriptions.[68] At present these trees are found in large numbers in the surroundings of Ajaigarh, Kalanjara, Mahoba and Khajuraho. Thus, we can say that during the Chandella period, thick forests with various types of trees existed. Similarly, we also find references of different types of gardens of fruits and flowers during the Chandella period. The Khajuraho inscription of AD 954 says:

> she bore to him that frontal ornaments of prince by families, the illustrious King Yasovarman who was a sword to (cut down) the Goudas as if they were pleasure creepers, measured the might of the Kashasa (and) carried off the treasure of the Kosalas; before whom perished the Kashmiri warriors, who weakened the Mithilas, (and) was, as it were, a god of death to the Malavas, who brought distress on the shameful Chedis, who was to the Kurus what a storm is to trees (and) a scorching fever to the Gurjaras.[69]

This verse of the inscription refers to both creepers and trees. The Khajuraho stone inscription of Kokkal of AD 1002 also gives the reference of creepers of good fame.[70] The creepers and foliage and trees are the favourite decorative elements of all the temples constructed during the reign of Chandellas. In the Nilakantha temple inscription found in Kalanjara,[71] the Ganga is described as a foliage banner fluttering on the pillar, that is, Siva along with Parvati as Salabhanjika. Grass-cutters are depicted in the sculptural art of Khajuraho.[72] This indicates that grass was used as fodder for animals. A number of sculptures in the Khajuraho temples depict a lady extracting a thorn probably vaguely representing one of the shepherd girls who had to go into the thorny bushes of the forests for grazing animals.[73] Flowers were used for many purposes during the Chandella period. They were used for the worship of gods and goddesses.

They were also used as decorative motifs in Chandella temples. The Chandella inscriptions refers to flowers invariably. Among flowers, lotus was very much popular as revealed in epigraphs and sculptures. The Khajuraho stone inscription of Kokkalla of AD 1002 gives information of tanks and lotus flowers in this way. "He who built tanks full of water, in which the lotus shone with the loveliness of the spreading rays of bright lustred moon, and temples high, like the peaks of the Himalaya, he, successful like Indra, was called Yasobala."[74] The Khajuraho stone inscription of Dhanga, dated AD 1002, refers to the beautiful lotus flowers:

> Glorious is (the god) with elephant's face (Ganesa), who, in his infancy, eager to snatch and eat up the white lotus stalks, extends his trunk again and again to the digit of the moon on the head of Siva and is struck by Parvati with the lotus flower as she shakes her head, feigning anger.[75]

Similarly, the same inscription also refers to garlands. The Khajuraho inscription dated AD 954 refers to spotless lotuses, 'lotus foot' 'worshipped with garlands' 'like a garland' and 'lotus-faces.'[76] These words give the significance of lotus flower. Thus, references of lotus in Chandella inscriptions and depiction of lotus in various forms in sculptural art of Chandellas indicate its importance in religious worship.

The wildlife in Jejakabhukti region was very rich during the Chandella period. This fact has been revealed in the inscriptions and sculptural art of the Chandellas. Like the vegetational diversity, the wildlife here is also quite diverse and very rich. Tiger, panther, leopard, wild dog, wild boar, black bear, antelopes of several types, *nilgai*, spotted deer, *shambhar* and jackal, etc., used to be found all over the forests of the region. During the Chandella period, hunting became a very important feature of the ruling class as well as the aristocratic members of society, as revealed by contemporary literature.[77] The sculptural depiction of hunting scenes provides a visual representation of forests and wildlife existing during the time of the Chandellas. Wild animals such as the lion, boar, deer, antelopes, wild goats and wolves too are depicted. These animals are depicted in forests where hunting parties are shown.[78]

Besides being an important occupation, hunting was also a good recreation. To learn aiming and wielding of the weapons, it formed a training for princes and soldiers. The temples at Khajuraho provide us with a number of scenes related to hunting.

A stone panel in the museum of Khajuraho depicts some of the wild animals like the boar and the wolf. The other two scenes are of horsemen passing through a jungle; we may say 'a jungle' because of the wild creatures that are shown along with the horses and in between their legs. There are deer, wolf, a boar, bull and lion, etc. A boar and a hunting dog with another boar are shown once again along with four horsemen.[79] Among these jungle scenes may also be included a scene depicting three men, two of whom are armed with bows and arrows and one has an axe-like weapon resting on his right shoulder. In front of these three men are two wolves facing each other with their front paws uplifted as if resisting the man. Behind them is shown a horned deer looking back with his front legs uplifted. The deer is looking at a man who is also armed with a bow and arrow. It seems as if the deer is trying to escape for his life.[80]

A beautiful royal hunt is depicted on the base of Kandariya temple. The king's bodyguards are going ahead. There are two men riding on big horses holding the reins in their left hands. They are wearing high boots, but carry no arms. In between the hind and forelegs of the second horse, there is a small figure of a boar and the horseman is taking a dagger from the man behind him to kill it.[81] Thus, these scenes reveal the forests and wildlife during the time of the Chandellas.

Pl. 17. Gate of Kalanjara Fort, Kalanjara.

Pl. 18. Natural surroundings and tank, Khajuraho.

Pl. 19. Natural surroundings and tank, Khajuraho.

Pl. 20. Ajaigarh Temple, tank and natural surroundings, Ajaigarh.

Pl. 21. View of Ajaigarh Town from the Fort, Ajaigarh.

Pl. 22. Koti-tirtha Tank, Kalanjara.

Pl. 23. Inside view of Kalanjara Fort, Kalanjara.

Pl. 24. Decorated temple ceiling, Khajuraho.

Pl. 25. Decorated temple ceiling, Khajuraho.

Pl. 26. Decorated temple ceiling, Khajuraho.

Pl. 27. Elephants and horses with riders, Khajuraho.

Pl. 28. Camels with traders, Khajuraho.

Pl. 29. Marching elephants, Khajuraho.

Pl. 30. *Simha Sardula*, Khajuraho.

Pl. 31. *Sapta Mriga*, Kalanjara.

Pl. 32. Hunting scene, Khajuraho.

Animals were also associated with different religions. The animals as *vahanas* of gods and goddesses became a part of religious imagery. The *vahanas* were assigned according to the nature of their masters.

The animals were associated with the army. The sculptural art of the Chandellas presents various illustrations of army life related to war. The elephantry was regarded as a superior fighting unit in the army. The inscriptional sources give various references to elephants. Similarly, Muslim historians[82] also showed that elephants were very much used in wars during the time of the Chandellas. The elephants symbolised the strength and dignity of a king. The horses have been depicted in the sculptures as going in procession, which consist of sometimes horses only, and sometimes horses marching with elephants. Thus, animals played a vital role in army organisation during the Chandella period.

During the Chandella period, animals were also used for conveyance. The animals like elephants, horses, camels and donkeys were used as means of transporting heavy materials related to construction of temples.

Thus, the wildlife and animals played a significant role in various ways during the time of the Chandellas. We still find a good number of wild animals in Panna National Park. The wildlife is reflected in Chandella sculptural art as a decorative motif also.

The Jejakabhukti region is known for its variety of reptiles. The dense forests of *sal*, teak, *tendu, bel, bar, peepal, mahua,* mango and *gular* provide food for wild animals and shelter for animals and reptiles.

1. Snakes

The region is also known for its variety of snakes. Many of them are non-venomous and perform the useful function of controlling rodents. Only some species of snakes have poisonous fangs. Notable among them are cobras, including the king cobra, karaits, vipers, etc. The Khajuraho stone inscription of Kokkalla of AD 1002 says,

> Adoration to Siva, I adore the adorable coil of matted hair carried by the beautiful Vaidhanatha (which is) irradiated by the expanding terrible hood of hissing broad serpents, marked with the half-moon which is excessively shining, more brilliantly than the Sun (and) yellowish, when in contact with the line of flames of the fire issuing forth from his tremulous eye.[83]

This inscriptional reference mentions that Siva is bearing the serpent having a terrible hood. The serpent is closely associated with Siva. At Kalanjara, near the Nilakantha temple, there is a colossal figure of Kala Bhairava, 24 feet in height standing in two feet of water. The sculpture is 17 feet broad. It is mentioned by Abul Fazl as being 18 arbits in height.[84] The figure has 18 arms, and is ornamented with the usual garland of skulls, with snake ear-rings and snake armlets, and a serpent twined round the neck. In the hands are various objects, of which the most prominent are a sword, a bowl of blood, etc.[85] This image bears the testimony of Bhairva worship at Kalanjara. The Kala Bhairava or Maha Bhairava statue is grand in concept, gigantic in execution and remarkable in its terrific appearance. It is a unique contribution to Indian art and iconography. The study of this image is very significant from the point of view of its association with serpents. The serpents are depicted in the Siva images as ornament and his attribute. We find depiction of snakes in various types of Siva images found at Kalanjara, Ajaigarh and Khajuraho. The snake is also associated with Ganesha. At Kalanjara there are many sculptural depictions of *Samundra-manthana* (churning of the Ocean) in which the serpent Vasuki is used as a rope for churning the ocean. The Mount Mandrachal was employed as the churning stick and its end rested on the back of the cosmic tortoise. The story says that the gods were relegated to hold the tail portion of the serpent as a mark of their receiving inferior treatment from the *asuras*, who caught the head of the serpent by virtue of their being of elderly rank. After the churning of the ocean, first came out the deadly poison. Siva swallowed it on the request of the gods to save all the creatures. After swallowing the poison, he held it in his throat and became Nilakantha, the main deity of Kalanjara.[86] This is the main reason of depicting this Puranic myth at Kalanjara in several sculptures.[87] The serpent Vasuki is prominently shown in these sculptures at Kalanjara.

All the ancient religions have given a special significance to the snake. The coiled and intertwined snake represents a moment in the undifferentiated condition of creation on which human life rests. The snake is the symbol of this interconnection – swift, silent, limbless and deadly. The sign of transition is vital to man, who must be assured that this world is a cohesive unity: he cannot exist either in chaos or isolation. Thus, Visnu at the moment before the creation of the universe is depicted lying in a yogic sleep upon the serpent Annanta with the multiple cobra heads forming a canopy.[87] At Kalanjara we find near Ganga Sagar a colossal image of Visnu, 13 feet in height, reclining on the serpent Annanta.[88] There is also another broken colossal image of Visnu in the same posture at the same place. This shows that the serpent is also connected with Visnu. Similarly, the serpent is also associated with Krishna and his elder brother Balarama. The Kaliya Naga, who was polluting the water of Yamuna was forced by Krishna to leave the Yamuna. Thus, he made an attempt to keep the water of Yamuna pure. Similarly, the serpent is associated with the Varaha incarnation of Visnu. We find depiction of serpents in various images of Khajuraho and other places. The serpent is connected with Jain Tirthankar Parshvanath.

The Chandella artist has also depicted serpents for decorative purpose. We find a beautiful ornamental depiction of snakes at the Ajaigarh fort temple.[89] Thus, reptiles and serpents played a significant role in artistic creation and were associated with main religious cults.

2. Scorpion

Owing to the thick forest region, we find scorpions in large numbers particularly in summer season. In Chandella art we find the depiction of the scorpion in the temples of Khajuraho. At Khajuraho, more profusely than at any other temple site, we see female figures with a scorpion marked on their legs. The female figure, *apsara*, is undressing herself on the pretext of removing a scorpion. On this interesting theme, Dr. Desai has given her interpretation in the light of a pun on the word 'Kharjura', which means (1) a date palm tree and (2) a scorpion. The scorpion-bearing (*Kharjura-vahika*) female figure could be linked up with the word 'Khajura-vahaka,' the ancient name of Khajuraho.[90]

3. Godha

Godha is very common reptile found in the forests. We find depiction of Godha in the Parvati temple of Khajuraho. This is a small shrine. It now houses an image of the Goddess Parvati standing on an iguana (*Godha*).[91] The depiction of *Godha* is not common in Chandella art.

4. Crocodile

A large number of crocodiles are found in Ken River. There is Ken Gharyal sanctuary, 24 km from Khajuraho near Raneh waterfalls at the confluence of the Ken and Khadar Rivers. We find depiction of crocodile as a *vahana* of Ganga in Chandella temples on the doorjambs. Generally Ganga is depicted standing on the crocodile in female form. This is a very common decorative feature associated with temple architecture from Gupta period. The crocodile is also reflected in the *toranas* of Khajuraho temples. This unique decorative feature is found in Chandella temple architecture.

5. Tortoise

We find the depiction of Yamuna in female form standing on the tortoise. Generally this decorative motif is found on the doorjambs of the temple along with Ganga. This is also a very popular motif we find in the Chandella temple architecture. The tortoise is also related with the incarnation of Visnu. We find depiction of tortoise in the sculptural art of Khajuraho. At Kalanjara, we find depiction of tortoise in the *Samundra-manthana* panels. The churning stick and its end rested on the back of a tortoise.

NOTES AND REFERENCES

1. Bansi Lal Malla, *Trees in Indian Art*, Preface, p. xiii.
2. S.D. Trivedi, *Bundelkhand Ka Puratattava*, pp. 1-11.
3. *Ramayana* (Gita Press), 11.94.
4. A. Cunningham, *A.S.I.R.*, Vol. XXI, pp. 90-91.
5. *Ibid.*, p. 91.
6. *Ibid.*, p. 22.
7. R.K. Dikshit, *Chandellas of Jejakabhukti*, p. 11.
8. *Mahabharata* (Aranyak Parva), 3-83-54.
9. *Ibid.*, 3-83-53-54.
10. *Ibid.*, 3-85-13-15.
11. *Ramayana*, 7, 2/39.
12. *Mahabharata* ('Vana Parva,' 24, p. 54).
13. *Ramayana*, Chapter, 15, p. 35.
14. D.C. Sircar, *Selected Inscriptions*, pp. 59-61.
15. *Arthasastra*, II, Chapter I, p. 46.
16. *Ibid.*, Chapter IV, p. 57.
17. *Ibid.*, Chapter II, 51.
18. Rock-Edict, II, D.R. Bhandarkar, *Asoka*, p. 261.
19. V.A. Smith, *The Edicts of Asoka*, pp. 33-34.
20. Rock-Edict II, D.R. Bhandarkar, *Asoka*, p. 261.
21. *Ibid.*
22. A. Cunningham, *Stupa of Bharhut*, p. 29.
23. *Ibid.*, pp. 33-39.
24. *Ibid.*, p. 39.
25. *Malavikagnimitram*, Introduction (Tiwari trans.), p. 6.
26. F.E. Pargiter, *J.R.A.S.*, 1894, p. 200.
27. M.L. Nigam, *Cultural History of Bundel Khand*, p. 28.
28. A. Cunningham, *A.S.I.R.*, Vol. XXI, pp. 22-23.
29. M.L. Nigam, *Cultural History of Bundel Khand*, p. 28.
30. J.F. Feet, *Inscriptions of the Early Gupta Kings and Successors*, CII, Vol. III, p. 18.
31. H.C. Raichoudhri, *Political History of Ancient India*, p. 538.
32. D.C. Sircar, *op. cit.*, pp. 994-96.
33. *Ibid.*, p. 395.
34. *Ibid.*, p. 265.
35. *Mahabharata*, II, 31, 13-15.
36. D.C. Sircar, *Select Inscriptions*, p. 265.
37. *Brihat samhita*, XIV, Vs. 29-30.
38. J.F. Fleet, CII, Vol. III, p. 13 (texts and translation).
39. *Padma Purana*, 91/39; 92/1.
40. *Garuda Purana*, 81/18/19.
41. *Brahma Purana*, 2/146/1
42. *Garuda Purana*, 81/18.

43. *Padma Purana*, 38 / 15, *Kurma Purana*, 36 / 12.
44. *Agni Purana*, 109 / 23.
45. *Padma Purana*, 90 / 34.
46. *Skanda Purana*, 4 / 6 / 25.
47. A. Cunningham, *A.S.I.R.*, Vol. XXI, p. 22.
48. *Vayu Purana*, 23 / 204.
49. *Langa Purana*, 24 / 104.
50. *Padma Purana*, 39 / 54.
51. *Sivouprisha* (V.P. Kashi).
52. *Mahabharata*, 3-83-50.
53. *Ibid.*, 3, 85-15.
54. J.F. Fleet, CII, Vol. III, pp. 84-85.
55. *Agni Purana*, Chapter 7, 1-9.
56. *Ibid.*
57. *Epigraphia Indica*, Vol. L, p. 126.
58. *Ibid.*, pp. 125-126.
59. *Ibid.*, pp. 128-129.
60. *Ibid.*, pp. 141-142, Vol. 19.
61. *Ibid.*, p. 334, Vs 21-22.
62. *Ibid.*, pp. 137-47.
63. *Ibid.*, pp. 122-135.
64. *Ibid.*, pp. 147-152.
65. A. Cunningham, *A.S.I.R.*, Vol. XXI, p. 67.
66. *Ibid.*, p. 40.
67. *Epigraphia Indica*, Vol. XX, p. 130.
68. K.L. Agrawal, *Khajuraho*, p. 25.
69. *Epigraphia Indica*, Vol. 1, pp. 126-128.
70. *Ibid.*, pp. 147-152.
71. *Ibid.*, Vol, XXXI, p. 165.
72. Krishna Deva, *Temples of Khajuraho*, Vol. 1, p. 279.
73. Vidya Prakash, *Khajuraho*, p. 113.
74. *Epigraphia Indica*, Vol. 1, pp. 147-152.
75. *Ibid.*, pp. 137-147.
76. *Ibid.*, pp. 122-135.
77. Vidya Prakash, *op. cit.*, p. 75. fn.1.
78. Urmila Agrawal, *Khajuraho Sculpture and their Significance*, p. 192.
79. *Ibid.* p. 176.
80. *Ibid.*
81. *Ibid.*, p. 177.
82. Vidya Prakash, *op. cit.*, p. 84, fn 4.
83. *Epigraphia Indica*, Vol. 1, pp. 147-152.
84. *Ain-I-Akbari*, Vol. II, p. 29.
85. A. Cunningham, *A.S.I.R.*, Vol. XXI, p. 33.
86. S.K. Sullerey, *Ajaigarh Aur Kalanjara Ki Devapratimayain*, p. 13.
87. Kapila Vatsyayan (ed.), *Prakṛti*, Vol. 3, p. 148.
88. A. Cunningham, *A.S.I.R.*, Vol. XXI, p. 41.
89. S.K. Sullerey, *Chandella Art*, p. 34.
90. Devangana Desai, *The Religious Imagery of Khajuraho*, Foreword, p. xviii.
91. Devangana Desai, *Khajuraho*, p. 62.

5

Animals and Birds

The Chandellas were the rulers of Jejakabhukti (present Bundelkhand region of M.P. & U.P.). The region is rich in natural resources with flora and fauna that is set against the beautiful and picturesque landscape, which attracted the attention of even Rama.[1] The flowing rivers, the majestic Vindhyan mountains, the fecund forests, the trees with the green leaves and variegated flowers, most of them spreading an aroma of perfume all around, the colourful animals, whose every little movement suggests their habits and propensities, the birds on the wings warbling sweetly, even the butterflies with the tinted pattern on their wings hopping on every flower bunch for sucking nectar therefrom, have all been a source of joy and inspiration to the Chandella artists, who have had from the earliest times an abiding love for the environment around. In our country, the thought has been a rare and pure one by the very mode of approach towards Nature. The animals, no less than trees and plants, have been taken as friends and companions. The deer in the hermitage is one of the inmates treated with utmost affection, caressed and fondled, fed and looked after. The birds were not of any less concern. The cow is treated as mother feeding her children with milk from her udder. The elephant was considered a friend in many ways. The horse was loved almost as a companion. The Vedic hymns invoke the grace of the celestials for the welfare of the four-footed and two-footed animals as well as men.[2]

Chandella sculptures may firstly be divided in two sections,[3] viz.,

1. Stone sculptures
2. Rock-cut sculptures.

The stone sculptures were carved on the stone slabs brought by the labourers from nearby stone quarries. We find a beautiful illustration on one panel sculpture at Khajuraho, where a stone slab is depicted as being brought by the labourers and the sculptor is shown sitting and carving the sculptures.[4] This panel indicates the sculpture-making process at Khajuraho. The stone sculptures were mostly the component of temple architecture in Chandella art. Sculptures of this type are classified by Krishna Deva[5] into five categories. Devangana Desai[6] classified them into eight categories. Generally art historians accept the classification of Krishna Deva. The fifth or the last category of Krishna Deva is of sculptures of animals including the *Vyala* or *Sardula,* which being a heraldic and a fabulous animal, primarily represented a rampant horned lion with an armed human rider on the back and warrior counter-player attacking from behind. Different varieties of this basic type are known with heads of elephant, man, parrot, boar, etc. This most typical and popular sculptural theme of Chandella art is similarly related with deep symbolism.[7] The Chandella artist has also depicted the *Vyala* hunt, different types of animals, birds, reptiles and others for decorative purposes. We find beautiful ornamental decoration of snakes at the Ajaigarh fort temple.[8] A very rich fauna and flora finds its place in Chandella art.

The second section of Chandella sculptural art consists of rock-cut sculptures, which are less studied by art historians. The rock-cut sculptures were carved at Ajaigarh, Kalanjara, Mahoba and Deogarh. The characteristic feature of these is that they are independent and not part of temple architecture. We find depiction of animals and birds in rock-cut sculptures.

Much work has been done on Chandella sculptures by various scholars.[9] But no systematic analysis of the material contents of the sculptures related to animals and birds has been attempted so far. The only brief attempt made in this direction has been by the author in this book.[10] An attempt has been made in the present book to study the depiction of animals and birds in detail as reflected in Chandella art and architecture.

The Jejakabhukti region, over which the Chandellas ruled for more than sixth centuries,[11] is full of thick forest. It provided shelter to different types of animals and birds. This environmental aspect is very nicely reflected in Chandella sculptures in various types and forms. The Chandella artist depicted different types of animals and birds to decorate their temples at Khajuraho and other places in various ways and forms to enhance the beauty of their artistic creation. The depiction of animals and birds in Chandella sculptures is also related with contemporary political, socio-economic, and religious conditions prevailing at that time. It has also symbolic importance and is related with religious traditions during the Chandella period. The depiction of different animals in Chandella art has been studied under the following headings:

HUNTING SCENES

Hunting and the chase of animals have been related with human life from the earliest times. The representation of animals as found in the sculptures of Chandellas include hunting, man-animal fights, animal combats and pet-keeping. During the Chandella period, hunting became a significant part of royal and aristocratic society as referred to by the contemporary bardic literature.[12] Proficiency in the chase was considered to be an achievement.[13]

The depiction of hunting in Chandella sculptures provides a visual representation of this. Hunting scenes are carved in the narrow friezes of *jagati* and the *adhisthana*. One very beautiful hunting scene is exhibited in the Khajuraho Museum. In this depiction, hunting parties appear to have started after a great preparation along with a large paraphernalia which included several hunters, some mounted and some on foot. The hunting scene in the Khajuraho Museum has been graphically described by Stella Kramrich in these words:

> A scene of 'antelope sticking' with two of the animals impaled, while an antelope, a bull, a ram (?) and two others animals are taken on lead towards the impaled victims. A small animals snifis it a scroll device fill the surface. The bearded hunter and the younger ones following him carry bows, dart and sword. A smallish and kneeling figure in front allows the longbad of the one of the two smaller animals (?) to pass

between the legs of caparisoned bull. A peculiar device behind the main hunter and the bull and antelope's head. A horse follows the hunter. What is the story? This narrative relief in its composition does not essentially differ from early Indian versions. But the modelling, etc., of men and animals is particularly Chandella; plastically inert in this example, the volumes are stuck within their own weight. The marching rhythm, however, carved by these onerous shapes still has flux.[14]

In this scene, the hunters are shown going on foot and the tamed animals are held by them by means of ropes and bands. The purpose of taking trained animals was to attract the wild beasts.[15] Getting the smell of these animals, the beasts came out of their dens or bushes and were instantaneously attacked by the hunters. The dogs, with their highly developed sense of smell, could easily detect the hide-out of the wild beasts.[16]

Mounted hunters mostly used a spear for attacking the animals.[17] Whenever necessary they threw it at the fast running beast.[18] The hunter also carried a sword, but instead of hanging from the waistband, it used to be fixed on the left of the seat on the horse, and was used only in an emergency, when the animal attacked the hunter. Generally, several hunters riding on horses surrounded the animal from all sides and gradually narrowing the circle, pierced it with spears.[19] In one of the scenes[20] a horserider is chasing a boar with a great speed. His right hand is raised to throw the spear at the animal. On the other side, another hunter is ready to charge with bow and arrow.[21] After the beast falls, it is trampled upon by the horse.[22] This assures the death of the animal and gives courage to the hunting horses. The scenes of boar hunting are the largest in number at Khajuraho.[23] This indicates that boar hunting was the most popular and also possibly that the region was full of boars. Next comes the hunting of deer.[24] The birds were also hunted. Some of them were quite big and heavy, such as peacock.[25]

After the hunt was over, the party returned with the kill with great rejoicing.[26] The hunted animal was slung by its feet from a pole and carried home by two or four persons, depending on the weight of the animal.[27] Lighter animals were tied to one end of the pole and carried by only one person. A frieze in the Kandariya Mahadeva temple depicts a hunter returning with his animal, a peacock.[28] He has tied its beak to one end of the stick that he balances on his shoulder. Prithviraja Raso corroborates these modes of transportation, but it mentions other means also, such as carts, camels, elephants, etc.[29] In one of the depictions of the hunting scenes,[30] two men are depicted carrying boar tied to the middle of the pole, while a man with a bow is shown leading. It appears that sometimes the hunter used to employ labourers to carry the animal; since the persons carrying the animal do not bear any weapons, they cannot be hunters.

ANIMAL COMBATS

During the medieval period, animal combats became quite popular in the Rajput dynasties. There are many scenes of animal combat in Chandella sculptures. Duels between elephants or between a lion and an elephant were also depicted at Khajuraho.[31] Generally, in such scenes, only the participating animals are depicted. In a few scenes, however, some human figures also appear, but none of them can be recognised as a king or a person of an equally high status.

MAN AND ANIMAL COMBATS

At Khajuraho, a few scenes depict fight between man and elephant. The man though weaker in strength manages to resist the animal due to his smartness and intelligence. In some scenes, the man is shown engaged in a fight with an elephant who is fully decorated and has trappings. The man is seen charging with a spear.[32] Sometimes, a man is depicted as holding the tusk of the elephant and charging with a dagger or sword.[33]

ANIMAL PETS

The sculptures of Chandellas reflect that the people took pleasure in keeping pets, both birds and animals. The women liked to keep a parrot in their homes and passed their lonely time by talking with the birds. Many sculptures depict a woman standing with a parrot perched on her left wrist and holding a bunch of fruits in her right hand.[34] In some cases, the fruit is absent and women are shown standing only with the bird on their wrist.[35] Their expression shows that they are talking to the birds.[36] The cage is depicted in one rock sculpture at Kalanjara.[37] A small bird, perhaps a Sarika, is sitting on the back of the palm of a woman depicted inside the Jagadambi temple,[38] who is carefully trying to shield the bird from the wind or light with her right hand, which is held like a canopy over it. A bird is held in the left hand of the woman,[39] who is looking fondly at it with her right hand held in the pose of offering something to the bird. In another depiction, a woman is holding mangoes by their stalks in her right hand while on the wrist of her left hand is sitting a parrot.[40] Among animals, the monkeys were tamed and like birds they too were allowed to be quite free and were loved. They could freely roam about in the home. In a scene in the temple of Khajuraho, a monkey is depicted even in the private chamber of the husband and wife.[41] Here a couple has been shown in embrace with a monkey standing nearby. He is holding an iron crook, held by the man on the other side. The lady has turned slightly to see the mischief of their pet. In case of monkey pets also, it was the woman who took more interest and treated the animals with care and love. In a scene a woman is shown standing with a monkey climbing up her right leg.[42] The woman does not appear to mind this. In another scene, the monkey has climbed up her left thigh.[43] She is again unmoved, watching her pet's antics with amusement. Ultimately, as depicted in the temple of Khajuraho, the woman has taken the pet in her lap.[44] Depiction of domesticated animals like the horse, the bull, the cow, the buffalo, the elephant, the dog, the monkey, the goat, the ram, the deer, the camel and the ass shows that cattle rearing and taming was popular and also formed one of the occupations of the people. Similarly, birds like parrot, peacock, swan and owl in the hand of women give a glimpse of contemporary means of amusement and keeping of pets.

Thus, animals and birds were closely associated with environment as well as with the life of the people during the Chandella period as reflected in the Chandella sculptures of Khajuraho, Kalanjara, Ajaigarh, Mahoba, etc.

ANIMALS AND BIRDS ASSOCIATED WITH RELIGION

Animals and birds were also closely associated with different cults prevalent during the Chandella period. Animals and birds as *vahanas* of gods and goddesses became part of religious imagery. Mostly *vahanas* of gods and goddesses were assigned according to the nature of their masters. The depiction of animals and birds in the Chandella sculptures will be studied under the following headings:

1. Lion

The lion is a royal animal, the king of the forest. He has great royal qualities. He symbolises strength, power and dignity. The traditional picture present in literature and art is of a lion springing on the temple of the elephant; we find such a depiction of lion in the sculptural art of Khajuraho temples.[45] The lion is depicted in the Chandella art in various ways and forms. The lion is depicted mostly as a *vahana* of Durga in various places in the Chandella sculptures at Khajuraho and other places.[46] The lion is also depicted in some images at Khajuraho, as the *vahana* of goddess Lakshmi.[47] According to B.C. Bhattacharya,[48] Lakshmi can have the lion as

Pl. 33. Hunting party with animals, Khajuraho.

Pl. 34. Labourers carrying stone slab, Khajuraho.

Pl. 35. Sitting Nandi bearing a Siva Linga on his back, Kalanjara.

Pl. 36. Cow and calf, Ajaigarh.

Pl. 38. Mouse eating *ladoos*, Khajuraho.

Pl. 37. A couple with monkey, Khajuraho.

Pl. 39. Sahastra Siva-*Linga*, Kalanjara.

Pl. 40. Chatura Mukha Siva-*Linga*, Kalanjara.

Pl. 41. Eka Mukha Siva-*Linga*, Kalanjara (Rock-cut).

Pl. 43. Merki Bhairava, Kalanjara (Rock-cut).

Pl. 42. Nine-headed Maha Sada Siva, Kalanjara (Rock-cut).

Pl. 44. Merki Bhairavi, Kalanjara (Rock-cut).

Pl. 45. Couple worshipping Siva-*Linga*, Kalanjara (Rock-cut).

Pl. 47. Discourse scene, Khajuraho.

Pl. 48. *Darpana*, Khajuraho.

Pl. 46. Vyala figure, Khajuraho.

Pl. 49. *Nakha Kshat Nayaka*, Khajuraho.

Pl. 51. *Khadaga Nartika*, Kalanjara.

Pl. 50. Woman writing a letter, Khajuraho.

Pl. 52. *Darpana*, Khajuraho.

her vehicle but he further states that no such image has come down to us, Khajuraho however supplies the rare example. This image seems to be a rare example of the use of the lion as a *vahana* of Lakshmi.[49] At Khajuraho we find the depiction of Simhavahani Durga at several places.[50] We also find depiction of the lion as a *vahana* of Uma in the Uma Maheshwar images of Siva.[51] Similarly, in the Mahishamardini images of Durga, the lion is depicted as *vahana*.[52] At Kalanjara we find the depiction of the lion face in the cloth of Kala Bhairava image.[53] Thus, the lion is also associated with Siva images. The lion is also connected with Visnu. We find depiction of the lion in Narasimha incarnation images of Visnu. Visnu assumed the form of man-lion, and tore Hiranyakasipu with his claws at the lingering twilight forming the junction between day and night, himself seated on the doorsill of the mansion of Hiranyakasipu.[54] We find the depiction of the lion face of Visnu in the three-faced and four-faced images of Vaikuntha. Such images we find at Khajuraho[56] and Kalanjara.[57] Thus, the lion is associated with royalty and regal power.[58] Similarly, lion is also associated with power. The lion is also connected with the Jain Tirthankar Mahavira as his symbol.[59] We find the depiction of the lion in the famous image of Bodhisattva Simhanada Avalokiteshvara from Mahoba.[60] At Khajuraho we find several independent images of lions carved in the Laxman temple, the Visvanatha[66] temple and the Devi Jagadamba temple.

Thus, lion has a significant place in Chandella sculptures. It also symbolised power, royalty, and dignified position of Chandella kings. So far as cults are concerned, lion is related with major cults of the Chandella period.

Vyala (Mythical Creatures): It is originally derived from Persian art. This composite creature, with the body of a lion and the face of elephant, goat, parrot, or other animals and birds, was known in India from at least the second century BC.[61] Vyala enjoyed a great popularity in medieval Indian temples. It was considered to be a protective motif, and was depicted in recesses of the wall, and on the brackets of pillars, at Khajuraho.[62] A warrior is often depicted fighting a rampant Vyala. Silpa texts describe different varieties of Vyala images. The twelfth century text, *Aparajitprichcha* describes sixteen types of Vyalas with faces of different creatures,[63] and adds there are further variations due to their diverse body forms. At Khajuraho the Parshvanatha[64] and Devi Jagadamba[65] temples have a number of different Vyala figures on their outer walls.

2. Elephant

After lion, elephant is the most important animal which is associated with different religions. The elephant is a noble and inspiring animal, majestic in stature, yet gentle. He is the very embodiment of strength, and yet the greatest symbol of restraint. The elephant is the most self-sacrificing. The trumpeting of the elephant on the battle-field strikes terror in the enemy.[67] The elephant symbolised power, dignity, and royality, which is why they were considered as the royal vehicle for the king. Similarly, the elephant is considered the *vahana* of Indra, who is the king of deities. Elephant is also considered the *vahana* of Rudra.[68] He is also associated with Lakshmi and we find his depiction in Gaja-Lakshmi images. Such images we find in the Chandella art.[69] He is also associated with Ganesha. He has the head of the elephant. The elephant is also depicted in Gaja Samhara *murti* of Siva at Khajuraho.[70] The elephant is also connected with Indrani images of Saptamatrikas.[71] The elephant is associated with the symbol of Jain Tirthankar Ajitnatha. We find depiction of such images at Khajuraho.[72] The elephant is also related with Jain Yaksha and Yakshi images.[73] Thus, the elephant is associated with all the cults prevalent during the time of Chandellas. We find some independent images of elephants at Khajuraho. Elephants are also depicted in the Krishna-*lila* sculptures at Khajuraho.

3. Horse

The horse was a very popular animal during the Chandella period. The horse is depicted in Chandella art at various places in different ways and forms. It is associated with the Sun god whose chariot it drives. We find the depiction of the horse with Sun at various places.[74] The horse is also connected with the Kalki incarnation of Visnu. Hayagriva, the horse-necked *avatara* of Visnu associated with learning, who saved the Vedas from the demons, is placed in cardinal niches of the Lakshmana temple and the Vamana temple.[75] There is also a four-faced Vaikuntha, with an additional face of a horse. The horse is associated with Jain religion as related to Samvanatha the third Tirthankar.[76] It is also related with Jainyakshi Monobega.[77] At Kalanjara, we find the depiction of horse in the scene of *Samudramanthana*.[78] Thus, the horse is associated with all the religions prevalent during the time of the Chandellas.

4. Nandi

In Chandella art, Nandi is popularly associated with Siva as his *vahana*. At Kalanjara we find some unique images of Nandi bearing a *Sivalinga* or *panch-linga*s on his back.[79] We find the independent depiction of Nandi at Ajaigarh, Kalanjara[80] and Khajuraho. We find a separate temple of Nandi at Khajuraho in front of Vishvanath temple. He is invariably depicted as the *vahana* of Siva in Uma-Maheshwar images carved at Ajaigarh, Kalanjara[81] and Khajuraho. Nandi is also carved at Kalanjara in human form having a bull head.[82] We find various decorated Nandi images at Khajuraho. Nandi is also treated as a *gana* of Siva. At Khajuraho we find Vasu images having the face of the bull. Nandi is generally depicted in seating posture in front of the Siva temple. Nandi is also associated with Jainism. He is the symbol of Jain Tirthankar, Adinath. We find a temple of Adinatha at Khajuraho. Thus, Nandi is related to different cults.

5. Varaha

Varaha is associated with the ten incarnation images of Visnu. In the Chandella sculptural art, we find the depiction of Varaha in different forms. At Khajuraho there is a separate temple of Varaha in front of the Lakshman temple. There is a very big image of Varaha installed at Khajuraho. According to Devangana Desai, it is the most powerful icon of Varaha in India.[83] Here he is portrayed as *yajna*-Varaha, in animal form. This magnificent sculpture in the round is positioned in the centre of the shrine with space for walking around it in a circumambulation rite. This Varaha image carries on its body more than six hundred seventy-five miniature figures in twelve neatly carved rows. This figure depicts all the important divinities of the Hindu pantheon, including Ganesha, the seven mothers, the seven sages, the eight guardians of space, the nine planetary divinities, the river goddesses, the seas, the Rudras and the different forms of Visnu.[84] This Varaha represents the cosmic form, *Vishvarupa*, embodying all beings. There was also an image, Bhudevi, which is not available now. This image is related to the victory of Yasovarman.[85] At Kalanjara we find an image in black stone in animal form of Varaha; now it is broken.[86] There is also a Varaha image having human body and face of Varaha lying near Nilakantha temple.[87] At Ajaigarh we also find images of Varaha in both forms. There we find the family of small pigs; it is the image of Shashti.[88] Varaha is also associated with other cults. We find a face of Varaha in the Vaikuntha images at Khajuraho[89] and Kalanjara.[90] It shows that Varaha worship was popular during the Chandella period and it was also associated with the victory of the king.

6. Cow

The cow has been specially chosen as a celestial animal, a mother to all human beings, offering them milk and bringing them up as her offspring. In fact, she is even more than that in fulfilling all their desires.[91] At Ajaigarh we find the depition of cow and calf. It is mentioned in an inscription as Surabhi.[92] We find only this depiction of the cow in Chandella sculptures.

7. Buffalo

A buffalo is the very embodiment of sloth, so lazy that he almost looks a picture of patience, with birds pecking on him as he is almost unaware of it. He drives terror into the heart of people when in a fury, and is appropriately the mount of Yama, the lord of Death. The buffalo is a sign of ignorance, gloom and death.[93] A massive form of ignorance is represented as the demon Mahishasura. He is the very personification of death and deemed to die. It is this colossal and monstrous ignorance in the form of a giant with buffalo head that Durga attacks and kills with an arrow of light to discharge the world from enveloping darkness, thus assuming the title of Mahishamardini.[94] In Chandella sculptures, we find depiction of Mahishamardini at Khajuraho, having six, eight and twenty hands, killing Mahishasura.[95] We find the depiction of Mahishamardini at Kalanjara[96] and Ajaigarh.[97] Buffalo is also associated with the Jain Tirthankar Vasupujayanath.[98]

8. Dog

The dog is a faithful, brave and loyal animal. He is a great companion of the hunter. We find his depiction at Khajuraho in hunting scenes.[99] The dog is the *vahana* of Bhairava. We find his depiction at Kalanjara[100] with Bhairava images. At Khajuraho we find depiction of Bhairava with his *vahana* as the dog.[101]

9. Garuda

Garuda is the mount of Visnu. He is associated with great speed. Some of the early Chandella rulers, including Yasovarman, were devout worshippers of Visnu. The god who preserves the universe, Visnu is associated with royalty and regal power.[102] We find depiction of Garuda as *vahana* of Visnu in two types of Chandella sculpture. In the first category he is depicted in human form decorated with ornaments carrying Visnu alone. In the second category, he is depicted in the same manner carrying Visnu and Lakshmi together. This type of depiction of Garuda is found at Ajaigarh,[103] Kalanjara[104] and Khajuraho.[105] At Kalanjara, we find a depiction of Visnu on the Garuda connected with a Puranic legend associated with Visnu, Brahma and Siva.[106] He is also associated with the Jain *Yakshi*, Chakeshvari. She holds a discus in her hand and rides the mythical bird, the Garuda.[107] He is considered as the enemy of snakes.

10. Deer

The deer is the most gentle among animals. He suggests childlike innocence and is looked after with an almost tender affection even by sages who have no longing for any belonging in the world.[108] Deer is associated with Buddhism as well as with Jainism.[109] Deer is depicted as the *vahana* of *Dikpala* Vayu at Khajuraho.[110] We find the depiction of deers at Kalanjara in Mrigdhara associated with Puranic legend.[111] Deer is also depicted at Khajuraho in hunting scenes.[112] The poet in India is never tired of describing the beauty of the eye to which the most charming feminine painted deep dark collyrium is likened. Sculpture and painting in India have equally glorified this.[113] The *apasara*s of Khajuraho also are depicted using collyrium to enhance their beauty and charm.

11. Monkey

A monkey is the very embodiment of fickleness. A monkey is sometimes conceived as so friendly as to act faithfully for his master. At Khajuraho we find the depiction of monkey as a pet animal.[114] In the Rama incarnation, Hanuman (the monkey god) became his chief devotee. Some Chandella coins bear the figure of Hanuman on one side. At Khajuraho is found a large statue of the monkey-god with a short dedicatory inscription, dated AD 922, on the pedestal.[115] At Kalanjara, Ajaigarh[116] and Dudhai, we find Hanuman images. The monkey is also associated with Jain Tirthankar.[117]

12. Rat

Rat is the *vahana* of Ganesha. At Khajuraho and other places of Chandella art, we find several images of Ganesha with his *vahana,* the rat. At Khajuraho we find a beautiful depiction of a rat eating the *laddoos,*[118] which is also liked by his lord.

13. Camel

The camel is a funny looking animal, but capable of carrying heavy weight. We find depiction of camels in the Lakshman temple at Khajuraho.[119] Their depiction indicates the trade relations of Chandella rulers with the rulers of Rajasthan. It can be surmised that they were carrying the fine stones for carving the main images of deities. They are not related to any religion so far known at Khajuraho.

14. Ram

The ram is the *vahana* of *Dikpala* Agni. The latter is depicted at Khajuraho in different temples with his *vahana,* the ram.[120] Sometimes, the ram is also associated with Kuber.[121]

15. Donkey

The donkey was the *vahana* of Devi Sitala. He was the least appreciated among the domesticated animals. The donkey is also associated with Ravana. At Khajuraho we find the depiction of donkey-faced *Vyala* figure in Kandariya temple.[122]

The birds are also noted for their special traits. In Chandella sculptures, different types of birds are depicted at Khajuraho and other places. We find depiction of mainly the following birds in Chandella sculptures:

16. Parrot

The parrot is supposed to talk when trained, and repeat a listless record of words as taught without understanding their sense. In Chandella art, the parrot is depicted as a pet at Khajuraho. At Khajuraho we find the depiction of Vayal as having the head of a parrot.[123]

17. Swan

The swan is the *vahana* of Brahma. It is also associated as a *vahana* of goddess Saraswati. We find the depiction of Saraswati at Khajuraho.[124] At Kalanjara we find the depiction of Brahma on his *vahana,* 'hamsa' near the Nilakantha temple.[125] At Ajaigarh swans are depicted in the Ranga Mahal group of temples as decorative motif. This is a very beautiful decorative depiction; the 'hamsa' is also depicted as the *vahana* of Jain *Yakshi* and *Yaksha* images at Khajuraho.[126] Thus, swan is a very beautiful bird and famous for its justice.

18. Peacock

The peacock is a beautiful bird with the brightest plumage. The dance of the peacock is proverbial and well known, with feathers composing the tail shot up fan-like in a beautiful semicircular arrangement of great beauty indicative of joy. This is when the peacock is full of joy looking at the sky with dark clouds indicating rain. The peacock is also associated with Karttikeya, son of Siva and Parvati; he is a war god. We find the depiction of peacock with Karttikeya at Khajuraho[127] and Kalanjara.[128] He is also associated with Jain Yaksha and Yakshi images.[129] At present we also find peacocks in large numbers in Bundelkhand region.

Thus, we find the various types of animals and birds associated with the religious life during the Chandella period reflecting that the contemporary environment influenced the artists to depict these birds and animals in various ways in their sculptural creations.

ANIMAL SCENES ASSOCIATED WITH ARMY

The tenth and eleventh centuries represent one of the most disturbed periods of Indian history. The country was divided into different small states consistently fighting against each other. Army strength was not only the deciding factor for one's political supremacy; it was the means of survival. The Chandella kings were well aware of the importance of army equipment, which they themselves had greatly relied upon for establishing their kingdom. By this time, the Muslims had also made their headway into India and were constantly hovering on the borders of the Chandella region. Out of sheer necessity, the Chandella army was strong, gallant and well-equipped.[130] The Chandella artist could not remain unattached by the conditions of the time, and army life claims the largest number of scenes. They present various illustrations of army life related to the art of war. Such scenes are mostly found in the thin friezes running round the *jagati*, the *adhishthana*, the inner *pradakshinapatha* and those near the junction of the wall and roof in the *ardhamandapa*, the *mandapa* and the *mahamandapa*. The Chandella sculptors also show that their army consisted of elephants, horses and foot soldiers.[131]

1. Elephantry

Elephantry was regarded as a superior fighting unit in the army organisation. The number given by Muslim historians[132] also show that elephants were very much in use in war during the Chandella period. The Chandella sculptures at Khajuraho testify the same story. They contain the various scenes in which elephants are shown as moving in processions; sometime they were kept separate from the army but generally they are seen either with infantry or cavalry.[134] Sometimes they march also in mixed processions composed of infantry and cavalry.[135] The elephants at times led the military procession when the destination had to be approached through dense forests and by the rugged paths. In one of the scenes,[136] two elephants are shown with riders. The one in the front is uprooting a tree with its trunk. It is clearing the way for the troops. The elephants often moved between two horses with riders who were always there to rescue this precious animal in the time of crisis.[137] The sculptures generally depict two riders on the elephant, one on the neck and the other on the back.[138] Besides providing a stable and comfortable mount for warriors, the elephant took active part in destroying the enemy. In one of the scenes in the Chitragupta temple,[139] an elephant is shown twisting a soldier with its trunk to knock him on the ground while the soldier is making a desperate attempt to kill the giant animal with a knife in his right hand. The elephant rider is, however, seen falling downwards, being unable to withstand the jerking movement of the animal. The elephants symbolised power, dignity and strength. To give their due, they were lavishly decorated and ornamented.[140] The importance of the forts of Kalanjara, Ajaigarh and Mahoba and other places in the Chandella kingdom, is clearly evident from its political history. The whole history of the dynasty has centred round the historic fort of Kalanjara and, to a lesser degree, the fort of Ajaigarh. Time and again the fortune of the dynasty depended on the possession of Kalanjara. The extraordinary importance of forts in the Chandella state was due to the geographical situation of the country and method of warfare followed in that period.[141] The elephant was also associated with the forts. According to the description of Nizamuddin, we find the mention of thirty-five elephants in Gwalior fort and three hundred elephants in Kalanjara fort as given to Mahmud by the ruler of Gwalior and Kalanjara.[142] Thus, elephantry played a vital role in protecting the Chandella kingdom. We also find the mention of elephants in Chandella inscriptions.[143] Like their contemporary Kalachuri kings, the Chandella rulers also assumed the title of Gajapati.[144] The depiction of elephants in large numbers shows their importance and popularity during the Chandella period. Thus, the elephant is associated with Chandellas in various ways.

2. Cavalry

During the time of the Chandellas, cavalry was an important part of the army. They also maintained a good cavalry force,[145] and appointed an officer to look after the combined forces of elephants and horses.[146] In the hilly region of Jejakabhukti, the cavalry must have proved a boon to the army. The horses, fully caparisoned, have been depicted in the sculptures as going in procession, which consist sometimes of horses only,[147] and sometimes the horses marching along with elephants.[148] Being of the swiftest conveyance, whenever any news of revolt or border incursion was heard, the cavalry rushed to the spot, followed by other organs of the army. One sculpture depicts a horse and the rider running at top speed.[149]

A few sculptures show a horseman attended by a man with *chhatra* and accompained by the soldier with swords and shield.[150] He may be the king, the commanding prince or the chief of the army leading the army.

We find different types of movement of horses in the sculptures. They are sometimes shown as troting,[151] walking,[152] jumping[153] and galloping.[154] The horses of cavalry and those used in hunting are always shown equipped with bits and saddles along with stirrups. Thus, horses played a significant role in army organisation of the Chandellas; this is evident from various depictions of horses in the Chandella sculpture. The Chandella kings also appointed physicians to look after the health of horses, called *asvavaidya* in an inscription of Ajaigarh.[155] The Chandella kings also assumed the title of *asvapati* or *hayapati*.[156]

ANIMALS ASSOCIATED AS MEANS OF CONVEYANCE AND TRANSPORT

During the time of the Chandellas, animals were also used as conveyance. Generally, rulers and high officials moved around on the elephants and horses. Besides being a strong part of the army, the elephants could serve the purpose of comfortable means of conveyance and as an efficient means of heavy transport in time of peace. The elephant is considered as the *vahana* of Devaraj Indra; certainly it was also used by the Chandella rulers for going to the forts and thick forests. Though we have not yet noticed the depiction of kings in Chandella sculptures, but we find the depiction of kings and high officials using the horse as a means of conveyance. Animals like elephants, horses, camels and donkeys were used as means of transport for carrying heavy materials related to the construction of temples and other things related to the needs of the general public. We have references in Chandella inscriptions of wealthy Jain traders who also played a vital role in the construction of temples during the time of the Chandellas.[157] The carts were also used for transporting the goods from one place to another. The bullocks must have been needed for driving these carts because it was a very popular means of transport in India in ancient times though, we have no such depictions in the sculptural art of the Chandellas. But a simpler variety of the cart is depicted in a Krishna-*lila* scene.[158] It is a two-wheeled vehicle with a yoke, intended to be drawn by a pair of bullocks. The notable feature of the cart is the set of solid wheels without spokes.

Animals were also associated with agriculture during the time of the Chandellas. Because cattle rearing is associated with agriculture, we have no such depiction in the art. Thus, animals played a significant role as means of conveyance and transport in Chandella period. They were associated in this way with economic activities and played an important role in the economic growth.

ANIMALS ASSOCIATED WITH EROTIC DEPICTION

The erotic depiction is divided in six groups at Khajuraho by Vidya Prakash.[159] The last group of this classification is related with animals. It depicts the coitus between human beings and animals. These types of depictions are noticed in the thin friezes in the *pradakshina* of Viswanatha[160] and Kandariya Mahadeva temple, and on the *jagati* of the Lakshmana temple.[161] The animal participants are the bear, ass, mare, dog, deer, etc.

Animals and birds, though associated primarily in Chandella art as decorative motifs, also reflect the contemporary environment, and various aspects of life during the Chandella period.

NOTES AND REFERENCES

1. *Ramayana* (Gita Press) 11, 94.
2. C. Sivarammurti, *Animals and Birds in Indian Sculpture*, p. 7.
3. S.K. Sullerey, *Chandella Art*, p. 31.
4. *Journal of Indian History*, No. 36, p. 34, fn. 2.
5. Krishna Deva, *Khajuraho*, p. 13.
6. Devangana Desai, *Khajuraho*, p. 29.
7. Krishna Deva, *op. cit.*, p. 15.
8. S.K. Sullerey, *Ajaigarh Aur Kalanjara Ki Devapratimayain*, p. 229, plate 13.
9. S.K. Sullerey, *Chandella Art*, pp. 17-22.
10. S.K. Sullerey, *Ajaigarh Aur Kalanjara Ki Devapratimayain*, pp. 183-184.
11. R.K. Dikshit, *Chandellas of Jejakabhukti*, p. vi.
12. Vidya Prakesh, *Khajuraho*, p. 75, fn. 1.
13. *Ibid.*
14. *J.I.S.O.A.*, Vol. 1, pl. xxii, fig. 9.
15. Vidya Prakash, *Khajuraho*, p. 76.
16. *Pritihviraja Raso*, 103-3.
17. Lakshmana Temple, *Jagati*, fz, backout.
18. *Ibid.*
19. *Ibid.*
20. *Ibid.*, fz, *op. cit.*, backout.
21. Vidya Prakash, *op. cit.*, p. 76, fn. 9.
22. Lakshmana Temple, *Jagati*, fz, backout.
23. Vidhya Prakash, *op. cit.*, p. 76.
24. Lakshman Temple, *Jagat*, fz, backout.
25. Kandariya Temple, *Adhis*, fz, rt out.
26. Vidya Prakash, *op. cit.*, p. 77, fz 1.
27. Kandariya Temple, *Adhis*, fz, rt, out.

28. Kandariya Temple, *Adhis*, fz, rt, out.
29. *Prithviraja Raso*, 125-56.
30. Kandariya Temple, fz, rt, out.
31. S.K. Mitra, *Early Rulers of Khajuraho*, p. 151; *Marg*, Vol. X, no. 3, p. 11, fig. 13.
32. Duladeva Temple, *Adhis*, fz, backout.
33. Lakshmana Temple, *Adhis*, fz, rt, out.
34. Viswanath Temple, backout.
35. Kandariya Temple, *Prad*, it, in.
36. Vidya Prakash, *op. cit.*, p. 76, fn. 3.
37. S.K. Sullerey, *Ajaigarh Aur Kalanjara Ki Devapratmayain*, p. 22.
38. Urmila Agrawal, *Khajuraho Sculptures and their Significance*, p. 165.
39. *Ibid.*
40. *Ibid.*, p. 166.
41. *Lalitakala*, Vol. 1-11, p. 31, fig. 15.
42. Vidya Prakash, *op. cit.*, p. 79.
43. *Ibid.*
44. *Ibid.*
45. Lakshmana Temple, fz, backout, *Marg*, Vol. X, No. 3, p. 12, fig. 13.
46. Urmila Agrawal, *op. cit.*, p. 60.
47. *Ibid.*, p. 58.
48. B.C. Bhattachary, *Indian Images*, Part I, p. 37.
49. Urmila Agrawal, *op. cit.*, p. 58.
50. *Ibid.*, p. 60.
51. S.K. Sullerey, *Ajaigarh Aur Kalanjara Ki Devapratmayain*, p. 105.
52. Urmila Agrawal, *op. cit.*, p. 62.
53. S.K. Sullerey, *Ajaigarh Aur Kalanjara Ki Devapratimayain*, p. 22.
54. T.A. Gopinath Rao, *Elements of Hindu-Iconography*, Vol. I, Part 1, p. 149.
55. Urmila Agrawal, *op. cit.*, p. 37.
56. Devangana Desai, *Khajuraho*, p. 41.
57. S.K. Sullerey, 'The Kalanjara Vaikunthapatta and its Historical Significance', *J.A.S.B.*, 89-91.
58. Devangana Desai, *Khajuraho*, p. 41.
59. K.L. Agrawal, *Khajuraho*, p. 98.
60. S.K. Mitra, *The Early Ruler of Khajuraho*, fig. 13.
61. Devangana Desai, *Khajuraho*, p. 40.
62. *Ibid.*
63. *Ibid.*
64. *Ibid.*
65. *Ibid.*
66. K.K. Chakravarty and M.N.P. Tiwari, *Khajuraho in Prespective*, pp. 166-172.
67. C. Sivaramamurti, *Birds and Animals in Indian Sculpture*, p. 10.
68. D.N. Shukla, *Vastu-Sastra*, pp. 144-145.
69. Urmila Agrawal, *op. cit.*, p. 58.
70. *Ibid.*, pp. 54-55.
71. *Ibid.*, p. 70.
72. K.L. Agrawal, *Khajuraho*, p. 98.
73. *Ibid.*, p. 105.
74. *Ibid.*, pp. 92-93.
75. Devangana Desai, *Khajuraho*, p. 41.
76. K.L. Agrawal, *Khajuraho*, p. 98.
77. *Ibid.*, p. 105.
78. S.K. Sullerey, *Ajaigarh Aur Kalanjara Ki Devapratimayian*, p. 144.
79. *Ibid.*, pp. 67-68.

80. *Ibid.*, p. 184.
81. *Ibid.*, p. 105.
82. *Ibid.*, p. 108.
83. Devangana Desai, *Khajuraho*, p. 41.
84. *Ibid.*, pp. 49-50.
85. *Ibid.*
86. S.K. Sullerey, *Ajaigarh Aur Kalanjara Ki Devapratimayain*, p. 150.
87. *Ibid.*
88. *Ibid.*, p. 27.
89. Devangana Desai, p. 40.
90. S.K. Sullerey, *J.A.S.B.*, 1989-91.
91. Sivaramamurti, *Birds and Animals in Indian Sculpture*, p. 15.
92. S.K. Sullerey, *Ajaigarh Aur Kalanjara Ki Devapratimayain*, p. 27.
93. C. Sivarammurti, *Birds and Animals in Indian Sculptures*, p. 16.
94. *Ibid.*, p. 18.
95. Urmila Agrawal, *op. cit.*, p. 62-63.
96. S.K. Sullerey, *Ajaigarh Aur Kalanjara Ki Devapratimayain*, p. 121.
97. *Ibid.*
98. K.L. Agrawal, *Khajuraho*, p. 98.
99. Vidya Prakash, *op. cit.*, 76.
100. S.K. Sullerey, *Ajaigarh Aur Kalanjara Ki Devapratimayain*, p. 22.
101. Devangana Desai, *Khajuraho*, p. 42. Urmila Agrawal, *op. cit.*, p. 56.
102. Devangana Desai, *Khajuraho*, p. 40.
103. S.K. Sullerey, *Ajaigarh Aur Kalanjara Ki Devapratimayain*, p. 154.
104. *Ibid.*
105. Urmila Agrawal, *op. cit.*, p. 43.
106. S.K. Sullerey, *Ajaigarh Aur Kalanjara Ki Devapratimayain*, p. 98.
107. K.L. Agrawal, *Khajuraho*, p. 103.
108. C. Sivarammurti, *Birds and Animals in Indian Sculpture*, p. 10.
109. K.L. Agrawal, *Khajuraho*, p. 98.
110. *Ibid.*, p. 111.
111. S.K. Sullerey, *Ajaigarh Aur Kalanjara Ki Devapratimyain*, p. 22.
112. Vidya Prakash, *op. cit.*, p. 78.
113. C. Sivaramamurti, *Birds and Animals in Indian Sculpture*, p. 11.
114. Vidya Prakash, *op. cit.*, p. 79.
115. S.K. Mitra, *Early Rulers of Khajuraho*, p. 193.
116. S.K. Sullerey, *Ajaigarh Aur Kalanjara Ki Devapratimayain*, p. 165.
117. K.L. Agrawal, *Khajuraho*, p. 98.
118. Khajuraho Museum Collection.
119. Vidya Prakash, *op. cit.*, p. 90.
120. K.L. Agrawal, *Khajuraho*, pp. 109-110.
121. *Ibid.*, p. 111
122. *Ibid.*, p. 117.
123. *Ibid.*
124. *Ibid.*, p. 88.
125. S.K. Sullerey, *Ajaigarh Aur Kalanjara Ki Devapratimayain*, p. 157.
126. K.L. Agrawal, *Khajuraho*, p. 105.
127. Devangana Desai, *Khajuraho*.
128. S.K. Sullerey, *Ajaigarh Aur Kalanjara Ki Devapratimayain*, p. 132-133.
129. K.L. Agrawal, *Khajuraho*, p. 105.
130. Vidya Prakash, *op. cit.*, p. 83, fn. 1.
131. *Ibid.*, p. 84, fn. 2.

132. *Ibid.*
133. *Ibid.*, p. 84, fn.5.
134. *Ibid.*
135. *Ibid.*
136. *Ibid.*
137. *Ibid.*
138. *Ibid.*, p. 85, fn. 2.
139. *Ibid.*, p. 85.
140. *Ibid.*, p. 86.
141. N.S. Bose, *The History of the Chandellas*, p. 134.
142. *Ibid.*, p. 60.
143. K.L. Agrawal, *Khajuraho*, p. 139.
144. N.S. Bose, *op. cit.*, p. 103.
145. H.C. Roy, *Dynastic History of Northern India*, Vol. II, p. 630.
146. Vidya Prakash, *op. cit.*, p. 87.
147. *Ibid.*
148. *Ibid.*
149. *Ibid.*
150. *Ibid.*
151. *Ibid.*, p. 88.
152. *Ibid.*
153. *Ibid.*
154. *Ibid.*
155. A. Cunningham, *A.S.I.R.*, Vol. XXI, p. 51.
156. N.S. Bose, *op. cit.*, p. 134.
157. A. Cunningham, *A.S.I.R.*, Vol. XXI, p. 67.
158. Vidya Prakash, *op. cit.*, p. 128.
159. *Ibid.*, p. 132.
160. *Ibid.*
161. *Ibid.*

6

Water Resources and Their Impact

Before studying the water resources of Chandella period, we must know the region over which the temples and monuments were constructed during the time of Chandellas. The boundaries of the Chandella kingdom varied from time to time but the area of Jejakabhukti roughly corresponds to what is now known as the Bundelkhand region of Uttar Pradesh and Madhya Pradesh. At the height of Chandella power in the eleventh century, this region was bounded on all the four sides by four rivers – in the north by Yamuna, in the south by Narmada, in the east by the Tamas, and in the west by the Chambal.[1] The Khajuraho inscription of AD 954 gives an account of the extent of Dhang's empire. It refers that Dhanga was ruling the earth "playfully acquired by the action of his long and strong arms, as far as Kalanjara and as far as Bhasvat situated (?) on the bank of the river Malava from here to the river Kalindi, and from here also to the frontiers of Chedi country and even as far as that mountain called Gopa (Gopadri) which is a unique abode of marvels."[2] Thus, rivers and mountains provided the geographical boundaries of the Chandella kingdom. The boundaries of the Chandella dominion, of course, changed from time to time. But they always included Mahoba, Kalanjara, Khajuraho and Ajaigarh, all of which are situated in the central segment of Bundelkhand.[3] These four places – Khajuraho, Kalanjara, Mahoba and Ajaigarh – comprised the vital centre of the Chandella kingdom.[4] The region was known during the sixth century as Chedi,[5] during the Chandella times as Jejakabhukti,[6] and since fourteenth century as Bundelkhand.[7]

We can divide the water resources of Chandella period in two parts:

1. Natural water resources
2. Excavated and constructed water resources.

NATURAL WATER RESOURCES

Jejakabhukti has a large number of rivers, many rivulets and beautiful waterfalls, which enhance the scenic beauty of this region. The small streams are usually tributaries and branches of big rivers. Sometimes, after rising from the mountains, the streams empty their water into a big river in lower course. There are numerous north-bound perennial river falls paying tribute to Yamuna River like Betwa, Dhasana, Ken, Bhagein, Paisuni and their tributaries. The *Puranas*[8] often enumerate the rivers as rising from the various mountain ranges. Of these rivers, the following may be located in the present Bundelkhand:

1. Yamuna

Yamuna is a famous river of India. It forms the north boundary of the Chandella kingdom. The Yamuna is regarded as one of the most sacred rivers of India. Devotees place it next to the Ganga. The Yamuna River is closely associated with Krishna. Ganga and Yamuna as river deities came into existence during the Gupta period in the temple architecture. The two ends of the temple's door lintel are adorned with the images of the river goddesses, Ganga and Yamuna, standing on their respective vehicles, the alligator and tortoise. This was a special attractive feature which originated in the Gupta period and for many centuries afterwards was accepted as the best decorative and religious pattern of a temple doorway.[9] It is most remarkable that Kalidas with his unusual power of observing contemporary art and life records the presence of the twin river goddesses Ganga and Yamuna as being in attendance upon the deity.[10] The literary description truly supports the architectural tradition.[11] This tradition of depicting Ganga and Yamuna in the temples was also followed by the Chandellas. The Khajuraho inscription of AD 954 refers to Yamuna by its other name, Kalindi.[12]

2. Betwa

Betwa is also known as Vetravati. The river Vetravati has been mentioned by Kalidas in *Meghaduta*[13] and also by Varahamihira.[14] Literally, Vetravati means containing canes. It has been identified with the Betwa joining the Yamuna near Hamirpur, Uttar Pradesh. It rises at the village Kumari in the Bhopal division and flows in a north-easternly direction passing by the ancient city of Vidisa (ancient Besnagar).[15]

The rivers Bes and Dhasan are among the important tributaries of Betwa. According to local tradition, the Pandavas fought with the king of Vidisa on the bank of the Vetravati.[16] The *Kadambari* of Banabhatta associates Malava ladies with Vetravati, surrounding Vidisa.

3. Dasarna

The river Dasarna is regarded as the same as present Dhasana flowing past Sagar between the Betwa and Ken. The river Dasarna was evidently named after the Dasarna kingdom mentioned in many works, including the *Mahabharata*[17] and the *Meghaduta*[18] of Kalidas. Dasarna has been identified with East Malwa with its capital at Vidisa.[19]

The *Kurma, Matsya, Brahmanda, Vaman* and *Vayu Purana*s mention that the Riksha range is the source of the Dasarna.[20] From the *Markandeya Purana,*[21] it appears that the river which has its source in the Bhopal region empties itself in the Betwa River. A Kalanjara inscription gives the title of Dasarnadhinatha to Chandella king, Paramardideva.[22]

4. Chambal

It is mentioned in ancient Indian literature as Charmanavati. Panini refers[23] to one Charmanvati River, the location of which is not certain. V.S. Agrawal, however, identifies it with the Chambal.[24] The *Mahabharata*[25] explains the name Charmanavati, as a rivulet which was originated from the skin (*Charman*) of the sacrified cows, i.e., from blood coming from the skins of the cows. A large number of cows are said to have been slaughtered at the *yajna* of

Rantideva. The *Mahabharata* informs us that the river formed the southern boundary of the Panchal territory.[26] It has also been referred to in the *Meghaduta*.[27] The river rises in an elevated point of the Vindhya. N.L. Dey[28] points out that the hill has three co-equal sources from the same cluster, viz., the Chambal and the Gambhir. The river, afterwards, flows down the northern slopes of the Vindhyan range, and enters Rajasthan at a point 193 miles from its source. Charmanavati is led by a large number of tributaries, both large and small. Among these, the Kalisindh joins it from the south, and the Mej and Banas from the west. Later on, the river passes through Uttar Pradesh where it ultimately joins the Yamuna. It forms the western boundaries of the Chandella kingdom.

5. Sindhu

The river Sindhu is generally believed to be identical with the river Kalisindhu, a tributary of the Chambal. The *Mahabharata*[29] possibly refers to it as the Dakshina-Sindhu, and the *Meghaduta*[30] simply as Sindhu as the river is called in the *Purana*s. Evidently, at a later period, the Sindhu came to be known as Kalisindhu which does not appear in literature. It takes its rise from a tank situated in the village of Nain, which was in the Sironj in Vidisha district of Madhya Pradesh. It flows in a north-easternly direction for about 150 miles through the Malwa region till it enters Uttar Pradesh, and joins the Yamuna.

6. Tamas

It is identified with the modern Tons flowing into the Ganga below Allahabad. The *Ramayana* mentions two Tamas Rivers, one of which flows about 10 miles to the west of the Sarayu. It was on the bank of this river that Valmiki dwelt.[31] The other has been placed in the Rewa region, and it falls into the Ganga near Allahabad.[32] The *Purana*s obviously refer to the latter as rising from Riksha mountain. The imperial Gazetteer of India points to it as the Southern Tons.[33] It rises in the Kaimur Range from a source known as Tamasa Kunda, near Maihar.[34] From here the river flows a north-easternly course for about 120 miles and after traversing the rough hilly country round Maihar, flows through the plain of Rewa region. Here it is joined by the Satna, and 40 miles lower down, it is joined by a few other effluents and spreading into a wide stream with long deep reaches, it enters Uttar Pradesh at Deora. After a north-easternly course of about 44 miles, it falls into the Ganga 19 miles below Allahabad. It forms the eastern boundary of the Chandella kingdom.

7. Ken

The Suktimati of ancient Indian literature is identified with the Ken, a tributary of the Yamuna, flowing through Bundelkhand. Cunningham[35] thinks that the name of Ken or Kayan is derived from the Sanskrit Kanavati. But this name does not appear in the *Purana*s. It seems peculiar that the name of Ken, which is a great river, should not be mentioned though it has its source in the same river shed as the Tons, Paisuni and others. According to N.L. Dey,[36] the river Syeni mentioned in the *Matsya Purana*[37] is the same as river Suktimati, and under phonetic rules Syeni would become Keni or Ken.

The *Mahabharata*[38] connects the river Suktimati with the Kolahala Range. The river flowed through the ancient kingdom of Chedi. Pargiter has placed the Kolahala between Panna and Bijawar in the Chhatarpur district.[39] It rises in the north-western slopes of the Kaimur Range and flowing north-east through Damoh and Panna, enters the Banda District of Uttar Pradesh near Bilharka. On the bank of the river stood a city by the same name (Suktimati of the *Mahabharata*,[40] Sotthivati of the Buddhists),[41] which was the ancient capital of the Chedi people.

The Ken runs through the Jejakabhukti from south to north, dividing it into two nearly equal portions, with the capital cities of Mahoba and Khajuraho in the western half and the great Forts of Kalanjara and Ajaigarh in the eastern half.[42] According to the legend connected with the origin of the Chandellas, the founder of the Chandella dynasty, Chandra Varman, was born on the bank of the river Kanavati, the modern Kiyan or Ken.[43] Thus, the river Ken played a vital role in the history of the Chandellas. It surrounds the famous Chandella fort of Ajaigarh.

8. Baghein

This is an important river of Banda district of Uttar Pradesh. It rises from a hill near Kohari of Panna district of Madhya Pradesh, and enters the Banda district at Masauri Bharatpur village. It flows north-eastward and at a point separates Banda from the newly created Shahuji Maharaj Nagar (Chitrakuta) forming boundaries between Atarra and Karvi towns. Continuing north-east, it joins Yamuna near Bilas village.

At the evidence of *Skanda Purana,* Avantya Khanda (Reva-Khanda),[44] N.L. Dey[45] identifies Baluvahini River with the Baghein River in Bundelkhand. The Baghein is a tributary of the Yamuna and the fort of Kalanjara stands on it.[46]

9. Mandakini

The Mandakini has been identified with the present Mandakin, which is flowing by the side of the famous Chitrakuta mountain.[47] It is a small stream flowing into the Paisuni, a little below Sitapur.

The river Mandakini along with the famous Chitrakuta has been mentioned in the *Ramayana.*[48] It appears that Rama resided for some time on Mount Chitrakuta during his exile.[49] The *Malavikagnimitra*[50] mentions a river named Mandakini. Its identity is, however, uncertain. But the author might have the river Mandakini around the Chitrakuta in mind. The river has also been mentioned in the *Brihata-Samhita.*[51]

10. Paisuni

Rising near the Satna district of Madhya Pradesh, Paisuni at the village of Mangawan falls from the Vindhyan plateau into five cascades, separated by a deep pool. The lower pool, which is always filled with clean, translucent water, is said to be very deep. This is associated with the legendary demon Viradh of *Ramayana.* From this point it enters the famous pilgrim centre Chitrakuta. It flows north-east almost parallel to Baghein River for some distance, then takes a turn to join Yamuna near village Kankota. The Puranic river Chitrakuta is identified with Paisuni by some scholars. The name of Chitrakuta evidently was derived from the famous Chitrakuta hill of the *Ramayana.* The *Ramayana*[52] associates the Chitrakuta range with two rivers, viz., the Mandakini and Malini. D.C. Sircar[53] thinks that the Chitrakuta of the *Purana*s is to be identified either with the Mandakini or with a part of it. But the name of the river Mandakini still survives, and Cunningham takes it to be the same as the present Mandakini, a small tributary of the Paisuni. So, it is possible that the Malini[54] is identified with the Chitrakuta itself, which according to N.L. Dey[55] is another name of the Paisuni. As the Paisuni was larger than Mandakini, we may think that it had a better claim to be called after the name of the mountain nearabout it.

Cunningham[56] found an allusion to Prasravana in Parisaroni or Paisuni, and accordingly, he identifies it with the present Paisuni, a tributary of the Yamuna between the Ken and Tons near the Chitrakuta. Prasravana literally means 'a spring, cascade or waterfall', and the stream, which is famous for the cascade, got the name of Prasravana *nadi*. In the same way the hill of Chitrakuta also came to be known as Prasravana hill.[57] So, it is possible that the Prasravana-nadi (i.e. Paisuni) in an earlier epoch was known as the Chitrakuta after the name of the hill.

11. Narmada

The Narmada is regarded as the lifeline of Madhya Pradesh. With a course of over 1312 km, this is the longest among the west-flowing rivers of Indian subcontinent. Originating from Amarkantaka, the Narmada flows westward through the asymmetrical valley of about 160 km in length entering the Vindhyas as on the north and Satpura on the south till it reaches down to the neighbouring region of Tripuri. The gorge-like valley is full of rapids and falls. At Bheraghat, near Tripuri, it forms the beautiful 15-metre high Dhuandhar waterfalls. Here the Narmada has a youthful appearance.[58] The Narmada also divides the Indian subcontinent into two culture zones.

It is also called Reva.[59] It was identified with the Narmada in post-Vedic literature.[60] The name of Reva, which has probably been derived from Sanskrit root 'rev' (to hope) owing to the leaping of the stream down its rocky bed, has been mentioned in the *Puranas* including the *Markandeya*,[61] *Meghaduta*[62] and the *Brihata-Samhita*[63] and epigraphs like the Mandasor inscription of Yasovarman.[64]

The Narmada is also known by a few other names as follows:

i. Daksinaganga mentioned in the *Skanda-Purana*[65]
ii. Induja[66]
iii. Purvaganga[67]
iv. Mekaladirja[68]
v. Mekalasuta[69] or Mekalakanyaka, possibly owing to its association with the Amarkantaka, which is a spur of the Mekla range, and
vi. Samabhava.[70]

Among the important tributaries of the river, the Banjar in Mandla, the Sher and Shakkhar in Narsingpur and the Tawa, Ganjal and Chotta Tawa in Hoshangabad are well known. The Hiran, another tributary, flows beneath the Vindhya hill near Jabalpur. Most of these rivers have a short and precipitious course from the hills.

The Narmada is regarded as one of the seven sacred rivers of India. The local devotees place it above the Ganga. The local legend avers that Ganga herself must dip in the Narmada once a year. She comes in the form of a black cow, but returns home quite white, free from all sins.[71]

The Pradakshina ceremony of the Narmada, that is to walk from its mouth to Broach to its source at the Amarkataka by one bank, and back by the other, is considered to be an act of great religious merit.[72] Every year a good number of pilgrims take part in it.

The importance of the Narmada also lies in the fact that it is generally esteemed to form the boundary between Aryavartta and Dakshinapatha.[73] The Narmada is the holiest river in Madhya Pradesh since the earliest medieval period. An early literary tradition regarded as Kumari originated from the abode of Siva[74] and testifies she was represented originating from Rudra himself. She was initially regarded as second only to Ganga in sacredness. She is also conceived as the Ganga of the south and another form of Ganga.[75] The Rewa inscription[76] of Malayasimha, V.S. 944 (AD 1192), invokes the Narmada as the virgin goddess which flows with pure sacredness of water from the abode of Siva, i.e., Amarkantaka and as one which removes sins merely by sight. Thus, in the twelfth century AD Narmada was regarded as a sacred virgin river goddess. The Narmada formed the southern boundary of the Chandella kingdom.

12. Waterfalls

The Chandella kingdom has a large number of waterfalls. These waterfalls are the natural water resources, which enhance the beauty of the region. The Khajuraho inscription dated V.S. 1011 (AD 954)[77] gives a very graphic description of waterfalls during the time of the Chandellas. It states:

> whose pleasure mount (was) that Vindhya the peaks of which are charming with the sweet notes of his excellences sung by Kirat women seated on spotless lotuses, (and) on which groups of peacocks are made to dance by the bubbling noise of waterfalls rushing down from its tops.

Panna district of Madhya Pradesh is famous for its diamond mines. Panna district having been one of the most thickly forested and a natural abode of the elephants at one time, has been a good source of perennial streams, picturesque waterfalls and natural reservoirs called *Kund* and *Seha*. Some of them are described below:

(i) Prapat Kund

It is situated near Panna town, not far from Padmavati temple. Prapat Kund is a waterfall associated with a deep water body called Kund. Jhiriya is another water body near Prapat Kund.

(ii) Pandav Prapat

This is situated by the side of Panna-Chhatarpur road, down the valley of the Ken River. Pandav Prapat is a beautiful natural fall which is associated with caves and *Jhirna*. This is a spectacular site.

(iii) Chiraipani Seha

This is situated in Panna district near Fatehpur, in the vicinity of Vyama River. In addition to the waterfall and reservoirs, this has numerous caves with rock-paintings.

(iv) Mata ka Seha

This is situated by the side of Panna-Chhatarpur road near Bhairo-Tek. Mata ke Seha is a picturesque waterfall and water body. There are also pre-historic caves and the protection for water which would have been important even in that period.

(v) Lakhanpur Seha

Situated in a deep forest setting, this is the biggest *Seha* also associated with pre-historic period; there are caves, rock-paintings and water-protection posts.

(vi) Brihaspati Kund

This is situated on the right side of Banda-Panna road before Pahadi-Khera, in the interior forest and on the bank of Baghein River. Brihaspati Kund exists as one of the most picturesque, deep and difficult waterfall associated with a deep reservoir of water with natural caves and old temples.[98]

(vii) Bedhak

A few kilometers downstream is Bedhak, which is a unique place, where the water falling from the top is highly siliceous and turns the wood of the trees into stone form.[79]

(viii) Raneh Waterfalls

This is situated 20 km. to the west of Khajuraho, on the river Ken, with a stunning rock formation in a variety of colours. This is a spectacular site.

EXCAVATED AND CONSTRUCTED WATER RESOURCES

Agriculture has been the main occupation of majority of people in India since the earliest times. The attention that the Chandella kings paid to irrigation corroborates this fact. They dug out wells, reservoirs and lakes[80] and raised embankments to divert the course of the rivers,[81] wells (*kupa*), reservoirs (*vapi*) and lakes (*puskarni*) of the Chandella period which still survive in Khajuraho and its vicinity. That works of public utility, especially those related to water resources, were extensively carried out by the Chandella rulers in their kingdom, is known from their inscriptions.[82]

There were several tanks and reservoirs constructed during the Chandella period throughout the whole kingdom. Their water management is very significant and it still serves the need of local people. The main reason for the construction of tanks and reservoirs was the shortage of rainfall. This fact is known from an inscription of Chandellas from Ajaigarh fort. It states that in the "Samvat year 1237 (AD 1180) on Monday, the second day of waxing moon of Ashadh, in the fort of Jayapura, for the use of all people, by the Raut Sri Vira, the Son of Tejla, a Kahatriya of the village of Kotia, during the time of famine, a bauli (well) was built on the road."[83] This reference also indicates that relief works were carried out during the Chandella period.

The geographical location of the Chandella kingdom was also favourable for the construction of tanks and lakes. We find a tank or some type of water source nearby a temple. The names of the tanks are also related with deities as Shivasagar, Ramasagar, etc. But some of the tanks and reservoirs were also associated with the name of their builders or the place where they were built. Some of the tanks, ponds, and reservoirs constructed during the time of Chandellas were located at the following places:

1. Shivasagar Tank

This is an important tank excavated at Khajuraho. The stone inscription of Dhangadeva of V.S. 1059 (AD 1002) records regarding the construction of this temple: "Sagar got it dug by his sixty thousand sons with great difficulty at the cost of their lives and subsequently that was filled with water by his three prominent grandsons; hearing this narrative of the origin of the sea, the wise king through a sense of competition, speedily constructed a lake 'Bilvarnava' larger than the sea".[84] This water tank is an important landmark in Khajuraho. The Shivasagar tank is possibly "the largest lake surrounded by towering temples", as described by Ibn Battuta, the Arab traveller who visited Khajuraho in AD 1335. At the time of Captain Burt's visit in AD 1838, and Cunningham's in AD 1865, this water tank extended about three-quarters of a mile to the north, along the area behind the Matangeshvara, Lakshmana, and the Vishvanatha temples. Cunningham mentions the Chitragupta to be on the west bank of the old bed of the Shivasagar and the Vishvanatha on its east bank. Nowadays this south-north bed has dried up and the tank only occupies the area south of the Matangeshvara temple.

The Shivasagar tank plays an important part in the ritual life of Khajuraho town. During the Shivaratri festival thousands of pilgrims bathe in the tank and then visit the Matangeshvara temple for worship of Siva. In the month of Kartik (November), women from Khajuraho come to the banks of the Shivasagar in the wee hours to worship Krishna.

Shivasagar tank increased the beauty of the surroundings of Khajuraho temples, particularly of western group. The Khajuraho stone inscription of Kokkalla of V.S. 1058 (AD 1002) refers to the construction of tanks, "He who built tanks full of water, in which the lotuses shown with the loveliness of the spreading rays of the bright lustred moon and temples high like the peaks of the Himalaya."[85] Thus, inscriptional sources give us valuable information regarding water resources.

2. Chopra Tank

This tank is located near the western group of temples at Khajuraho. This is a small water tank. It is a three-storeyed steeped tank. Its construction near the Sun temple, connected with the healing of diseases, is significant.

3. Khudhar Nala

Khajuraho is situated on the banks of the Khudhar Nala, a tributary of the Ken River. It surrounds the Khajuraho town. There are more than twenty big and small tanks at Khajuraho assigned to Chandella period. This indicates the richness of the water resources in Khajuraho during the Chandella period.

4. Tanks of Mahoba

Mahoba is a historic city of the Chandellas. The Chandellas who were great builders, left behind an extraordinary legacy of temples and tanks. The lakes constructed by the Chandellas are an extraordinary creation of engineering skill and successful water management systems. These lakes were formed by building massive embankments across shallow valleys. The lakes include Rahila Sagar built by the fifth Chandella ruler Rahila, the Kirti Sagar, built by Chandella ruler Kirtivarman and Vijay Sagar, built by the Chandella ruler Vijayapala. The Madan Sagar built by Madanvarman Chandella, is a picturesque sight.

Besides the tanks, Mahoba has two famous *Kunds* of Chandella period lined with granite slabs in reverse pyramid shape. Rama Kunda is located to the west of Madan Sagar, while Suraj Kund is located near Rahila Sagar.

5. Tanks and Ponds of Kalanjara

The famous fort of Kalanjara played a very significant role in the history of the Chandellas. There are many tanks and rock-cut water ponds constructed here. Some of them are described below:

(i) Bhairava Kund

This is located near the sixth gate of Kalanjara fort. To the west of this gate is the Raoni. Immediately above the Bhairava Kund, there is a colossal figure of Bhairava cut in the rock. This *kund* has water and due to its relation with Bhairava image, it is named as Bhairava Kund. Here also are two figures of pilgrims represented carrying water in the usual manner in two vassels fixed to the end of a Banghi pole.

(ii) Patal Ganga

The Patal Ganga is a large deep well or reservoir, cut in the rock. The water is deep, and is constantly dripping and trickling from the roof and sides. Due to its deep water, it was named Patal Ganga.

(iii) Pandu Kund

Pandu Kund is a shallow circular basin, about 12 feet in diameter, into which the water is constantly trickling from the crevices in the horizontal strata of rock. This *kund* is very old.

(iv) Budhi or Burhiya Tal

Near the middle of the east face, there is a natural hollow, in the bottom of which has been excavated in the rock a small reservoir with steps all round. This is called the Budhi or Burhiya Tal. Its waters are believed to possess great healing power, as the leprous Raja Kirtivarman, after having bathed in the tank, found himself healed.

(v) Mrig-dhara

Near the middle of the south face is the Mrig-dhara or 'Antelope's spring', a small pool in an inner chamber of the rampart into which water is constantly trickling. It is no doubt supplied from the great reservoir of Kot-tirth on the high ground nearby this place associated with the Puranic stories.[86]

(vi) Kot-tirth

This is large reservoir with several flights of steps and many remains of sculptures. Kot-tirth, or the 'Fort-Holy Place', is the chief object of pilgrimage in Kalanjarā. In the south-east corner, there is said to be a deep hole, and this was the original holy pool of the place, which was eventually enlarged to the present size. This name is also written as Koti-tirth or the 'ten million places of pilgrimage', and Kot-tirth or the 'lepers' where lepers are cured by bathing.

6. Swarga Rohina Kund

Just outside the *mandapa* of Nilakantha temple there is a deep *kund* or rock-cut reservoir, called Swarga Rohina. This is the main source for Nilakantha. Generally, pilgrims after taking bath visit the Nilakantha temple at Kalanjara.

7. Ganga Sagar or Shivasuri Ganga

On the north face of the hill, and about 60 or 70 feet above the plain, there is a fine stone-walled tank called Ganga Sagar or Shivasuri Ganga, 160 feet in length and 120 feet in breadth. It has a continuous flight of steps on three sides, and only a narrow flight in the middle of the fourth side. A long flight of steps lands to the top of the embankment. The whole of the steps and walls are formed of cut stones, including numerous carved pillars, bracket capitals, and broken statues. On this site there had once been a very fine temple, as shown not only by their remains, but also by a colossal figure of Visnu, 13 feet in length reclining on the serpent Ananta. It seems that the tank was referred to in the *Mahabharata*.[87]

8. Tanks of Ajaigarh

Ajaigarh is the famous fort of the Chandellas. But the name of Ajaigarh is not found in any of the inscriptions, the name being invariably given as Jayapura-durga, or the Fortress of Jayapura.[88] During the time of Chandellas, there were many tanks and ponds constructed by the Chandella rulers and their officials. Some of them are described here:

(i) Ganga-Jamna Tanks

Near the northern gate, there are two tanks excavated from the rock, which are known by the name of Ganga-Jamna. Almost exactly in the same size, these tanks were excavated during the time of the Chandella king Viravarman. An inscription inscribed on the front part of a rock forming the roof the tanks records the construction a *nijara-kupa* and *prapra* at Ajaigarh and of a tank and a hall at Nandipura by Viravarman's chief queen Kalyanadevi.[89]

(ii) Ajaypal-Ka-Talao

Almost exactly in the middle of the fort, there is a large tank cut in the rock called Ajaypal-Ka-Talao. The tank is an irregular excavation in the solid rock; it is greatly longer and appears to have been the natural result of excavations made to obtain material for building. It is said that it never dried up, but always had a depth of ten feet of water in the deepest part. This tank plays an important part in the ritual life of Ajaigarh town. During the Makar Sankranti festival, thousands of pilgrims bathe in the tank and head for the Ajaipal temple for worship.

(iii) Parmar Tal

Near the southern end of the fort, there is a another tank called Parmar Tal, or the reservoir of Raja Parmal. The tank is not large, but is said to be very deep; its sides are supported by massive vertical stone walls with *ghats;* the walls diminish upwards by narrow steps, the steps of the *ghat* are large and broad; on a slab on one of the steps of the *ghat* there is an inscription. Close by there is a ruined temple of the Chandella times which is also attributed to Raja Parmal; and at a short distance there are two other temples standing together known as Chandella Mahal.

SIGNIFICANT WATER WORKS

The undertaking of the works of public utility was highly recommended by thinkers from very earliest times. *Vishnu Dharmasastra* records that "one who digs a well for the public is saved from the fruits of half his sins when the water has begun to flow forth".[90] Bana Bhatta mentioned that the *Smriti*s enjoined upon men the foundation for public use of halls, shelters, wells, gardens, embankments, etc.[91] Some writers even say that the reward of sacrifices is only heaven, but by *purta,* i.e., consecration of temples, tanks and gardens, one is released from *samsara.*[92] This indicates that charitable works for the use of the public or large sections of the public came to be regarded as more meritorious than sacrifices, in the gifts of which only the Brahmanas benefited.[93]

According to the *Smritis,* water reservoirs dug out by men are of four kinds, viz., *Kupa, Vapi, Puskarni* and *Tadaga. Kupa* is usually defined as a well of five to fifty cubit in length. *Vapi* is a well with a flight of step on all sides or on three, two or one side only and its length varies from 50 to 100 cubits. A Puskarni (pond) is between 100 to 200 cubits in length or diameter, and *Tadaga* is from 200 to 800 cubits.[94] The Chandella inscriptions record the construction of all kinds of water reservoirs. Sukra says that the king should see to the adequate supply of water in the country by digging wells, wells with steps, tanks, lakes, etc.[95] The great attention paid by the Chandella kings to this problem is testified by the number of tanks and lakes that still exist in the different parts of Chandella kingdom.

IMPACT OF WATER RESOURCES

All works on architecture contain long chapters on the *Bhuparkasha* or the examination of the soil. In these chapters lands are directed to be examined as regards their colour, taste, fragrance, fertility, elevation and even the surrounding scenery. This shows the significance attached by the Indians to the site of a temple. A passage from the work of Kasyapa, a predecessor of Varahamihira, is quoted by Bhottotpala, according to which, "A place where tanks full of sweet and transparent water, thronged with birds, abound, where forest and pleasure gardens are in numbers, where trees always blossom, where swans and karandava birds live in flocks and where peacocks dance – there the gods always remain and enjoy pleasure."[95] The best place for constructing a temple was, therefore, on the seashore, on a river, on the skirt of a forest and on a hill, beside a spring. The Khajuraho and the other temples prove that Chandellas always followed this practice in building a temple. Varahamihira while discussing the subject adds, "The gods come near the places which have water and gardens either natural or artifical."[97] It is therefore evident from this passage that in crowded cities and towns where the natural scenery was not very attractive, where rivers or forests were not available, temples were built on the bank of tanks and flower gardens were made to render the place beautiful and attractive to the gods. All Chandella temples, ruined or existing, are thus found to have tanks near them.

It is therefore very probable that the artists did not stop with merely the excavation of tanks or the foundation of a garden by the side of a temple. Scenes from nature, creeper and foliage, peacocks and swans, herds of elephants and monkeys are the favourite decoration of all the temples found in Chandella kingdom. A description in the *Samaranga Sutradhara* of the figure to be carved on building points to these facts. This tendency of making the site attractive according to the direction of the *Silpasastra*s is thus apparent from the text as well as the decoration of the temples themselves.[98]

Thus, the water resource makes the temple's site attractive and creates a scenic beauty. The water resources around the temple also create an atmosphere of purity and spirituality. Water resources are closely associated with religious rituals. Before visiting the temple generally people take bath and then they visit the temple and worship the deity. Thus, water played a significant part in the ritual life of temples during the time of the Chandellas. No daily, monthly or annual ceremony is complete without ritual purification with water. At birth, marriage and death this concept is articulated.

It is water that sustains life, the first principle of fertility and of life whether of ocean or river or clouds or sky. The archaeological evidence of Mohenjodaro, Harrappa, Lothal and recent excavations at Ganga Valley leave no doubt about the fundamental ritual importance accorded to water and its fecundity. The Vedas devote many hymns to water.[99] Inscriptional sources connected with different dynasties throw valuable light on the water resources. Similarly, Chandella inscriptions also throw light on the significance of water resources. The construction of water resources is considered a holy work.

The water resources influence the physical and mental activities of artists. The rivers, tanks, gardens and aquatic animals are reflected in Chandella art and architecture by various ways and means. The numerous art motifs and decorative patterns and designs are taken from water resources surrounding the temple complex. Of aquatic animals, mention is made of alligators capable of devouring elephants, which find a very significant place in Chandella art as *vahana* of river deity Ganga. The Chandella sculptor carved the *torana*s of the temple archways with decorative motifs of *Makaratorana*s very beautifully and artistically, which is a rare motif found generally in Chandella temples only. The tortoise also finds place in Chandella temple as *vahana* of Yamuna and as one of the incarnations of Visnu. The tortoise is also depicted in scenes of *Samudramanthana* in the sculptural art of Kalanjara. The fish also finds its place in the form of Visnu incarnation. We also find depiction of fish in some sculptures of Kalanjara. Similarly, swans are depicted on the doors of Chandella temples at Ajaigarh fort.

The lotus flourishes in the water. In mythical terms, the lotus emerges from primeval water, whether river or pond. It is the most important of vegetative form born of water, connected to the mythical centre of the earth through its stem, and always above the water, its leaves the symbol of untainted purity, its flowers blossoming with fragrance. Physically, the lotus is a typical ecological statement of the processes of nature. Symbolically, it assumes the greatest importance in Indian myth, art and ritual.[100]

All lotuses, whether as seat (*asana*), as emblem or epithet, denote fecundity, abundance and well-being. Logically, lotus becomes goddess and is personified as Sri and Lakshmi. She is praised as lotus-born (*Padmasana bhava* or *Padmaja*), standing on lotus (*Padmasthita*), lotus-coloured (*Padmavaran*), lotus thighed (*Padma-ura*), lotus-eyed (*Padmakshi*), abounding in lotus (*Padmini*), decked with lotus garlands (*Padmamalini*) and a thousand other names.[101] We are familiar with Goddess Sarasvati, also associated with lotus. Lotus is also associated with Visnu as he holds lotus as *ayudha* in his hands. Similarly, lotus originated from the navel of Visnu and Brahma sits on the lotus to create the world. Lotus is also connected with the Sun. Similarly, lotus is associated with Bodhisattava Padmapani and is also connected with Jain Tirthankars. The Chandella artist also utilised the lotus to decorate the ceiling of the *mandapas*. Thus, water-born lotus finds a place in Chandella art and architecture in various forms of decorative motifs.

There are a number of panels in Khajuraho temples which exhibit in their small friezes the various prevalent modes of worship. The most complete is the one found lying on the bank of the Shivasagar lake; now it is preserved in the museum. All of these *puja* scenes depict Siva in his *linga* form. These *puja* scenes show that *linga* is placed on a high pedestal and a worshipper is shown pouring water over the *linga*. Thus, these scenes depict the utility of water in worship of Siva.

At Kalanjara, there are many scenes of water carriers carved in the rocks. These images of water carriers also throw light on the significance of water in those days. In assessing the impact of water resources in Chandella art and architecture, we must consider the vital part played by the water resource shaping an amicable environment for worship and creation of the site as recommended in the canons of Indian architecture.

The flowing rivers, the tanks with flowering lotuses, the majestic Vindhyan mountains, the fecund forests, the trees with green leaves and variegated flowers, most of them spreading an aroma of fragrance all around, the colourful animals, the birds on the wings warbling sweet songs, even the butterflies with painted patterns on their wings hopping on every flower bunch for sucking nectar therefrom, have all been a source of joy and inspiration to the Chandella artists, who have had from the earliest times an abiding love for the environment around.

NOTES AND REFERENCES

1. R.K. Dikshit, *Chandellas of Jejakabhukti*, pp. 10-11; Devangana Desai, *Khajuraho*, p. 8.
2. *Epigraphia Indica*, Vol. I, pp. 129, 134, V. 45.
3. S.K. Mitra, *Early Rulers of Khajuraho*, p. 6.
4. N.S. Bose, *History of the Chandellas*, p. 13.
5. *Journal of the Asiatic Society of Bengal – (1895)*, p. 38.
6. *Epigraphia Indica*, Vol. I, p. 47.
7. R.K. Dikshit, *op. cit.*, p. 12, fn. 3.
8. P.K. Bhattacharya, *Historical Geography of Madhya Pradesh*, p. 84, fn. 7.
9. V.S. Agrawala, *Studies in Indian Art*, pp. 220-221.
10. *Ibid.*
11. *Ibid.*
12. *Epigraphia Indica*, Vol. I, p. 146, V. 55.

13. *Meghaduta*, 1, 25.
14. *Brihatasamhita*, XVI, 9.
15. *Imperial Gazetteer of India*, Vol. VIII, p. 17.
16. *Ibid.*
17. *Mahabharata*, II, Ch.33.
18. *Meghaduta*, I, 25-26.
19. P.K. Bhattacharya, *op. cit.*, p. 100, fn. 9.
20. H.G. Raychaudhuri, *Studies in Indian Antiquities*, 1958, p. 109.
21. *Markandeya Purana*, Ch. 57 (ed. Pargiter).
22. A. Cunningham, *A.S.I.R.*, Vol. XXI, pp.37-38.
23. Panini, *Astadhyayi*, VIII, 2, 12.
24. V.S. Agrawala, *Indian as Known to Panini*, p. 47.
25. *Mahabharata*, VII, Ch. 67.
26. *Ibid.*, I, Ch. 140.
27. *Meghaduta*, I, 46.
28. N.L. Dey, *Geographical Dictionary of Ancient and Mediaeval India*, S.V. Charmanavati.
29. *Mahabharata*, III, Ch. 82.
30. *Meghaduta*, I, 30.
31. *Ramayana*, I, Ch. 2.
32. *Ibid.*, II, Ch. 46.
33. *Imperial Gazetteer of India*, Vol. XXIII, p. 410.
34. P.K. Bhattacharya, *op. cit.*, p. 102, fn. 6.
35. A. Cunningham, *A.S.I.R.*, Vol. XXI, p. 78.
36. N.L. Dey, *op. cit.*, S.V. Syeni.
37. *Matsaya Purana*, Ch.113, V. 25.
38. *Mahabharata*, I, Ch. 63.
39. H.G. Raychaudhuri, *op. cit.*, p. 118.
40. *Mahabharata*, 111, Ch 22.
41. P.K. Bhattacharya, *op. cit.*, p.106, fn. 8.
42. A. Cunningham, *A.S.I.R.*, Vol. XXI, p. 78.
43. *Ibid.*, p. 79.
44. P.K. Bhattacharya, *op. cit.*, p. 104.
45. *Ibid.*, p. 104, fn.9.
46. *Ibid.*, p. 104, fn. 10.
47. A. Cunnigham, *A.S.I.R.*, Vol. XXI, p. 11.
48. P.K. Bhattacharya, *op. cit.*, p. 100, fn. 2.
49. *Ibid.*, fn. 3.
50. *Ibid.*, fn. 4.
51. *Brihatasamhita*, XVI, 10.
52. *Ibid.*, p. 101, fn. 6.
53. *Ibid.*, fn. 7.
54. *Ibid.*
55. N.L. Dey, *op. cit.*, p. 50.
56. A. Cunningham, *A.S.I.R.*, Vol. XXI, pp. 10-12.
57. P.K. Bhattacharya, *op. cit.*, p. 102, fn. 2.
58. V.S. Pathak and S.K. Sullerey, 'Tripuri Tirthapatta: A Sculptural Mythic Represention of Tripuri', *Art of Kalachuris*, p. 17.
59. The earliest reference to the Reva may be found in *Satpath Brahman*, XII. S.I 17, I.3.1.
60. P.K. Bhattacharya, *op. cit.*, p. 96, fn. 2.
61. *Markandeya Purana*, IV. 29.
62. *Meghaduta*, I. 19.
63. *Brihatasamhita*, XII, 6.

64. *Corpus Inscriptionum Indicarum*, Vol. III, p. 139.
65. *Skanda Purana*, Revakhand, Ch. 4.
66. P.K. Bhattacharya, *op. cit.*, p. 96, fn.13.
67. *Ibid.*, fn. 14.
68. *Ibid.*, fn. 15.
69. *Epigraphia Indica*, Vol. IV, p. 280.
70. P.K. Bhattacharya, *op. cit.*, p. 97, fn. 1.
71. *Ibid.*, p. 99, fn. 2.
72. *Ibid.*, fn. 4.
73. *Matsya Purana*, CLXXXVIII, 97.
74. Chakravarti and R K. Sharma, *Art of Kalachuris*, p. 51.
75. *Skanda Purana* IV.
76. *M.A.S.I.*, XXIII, p. 133.
77. *Epigraphia Indica*, Vol. I, pp. 125-26, 131, V. 13.
78. Prakas Bhartandu *et al.*, *Problems and Potentials of Bundelkhand*, p. 101.
79. *Ibid.*
80. *Epigraphia Indica*, Vol. 1, pp. 325-330.
81. *Epigraphia Indica*, Vol. 1, p. 144, V. 38.
82. N.S. Bose, *op. cit.*, p. 146.
83. A. Cunningham, *A.S.I.R.*, Vol. XXI, p. 50.
84. *Epigraphia Indica*, Vol. I, p. 144, V. 38.
85. *Ibid.*, pp. 147-152.
86. S.K. Sullerey, *Ajaigarh Aur Kalanjara Ki Divyapratimayain*, pp. 13-14.
87. *Ibid.*, p. 10, fn.1.
88. *Ibid.*, p. 22, fn.2.
89. *Epigraphia Indica*, Vol. I, pp. 328.
90. N.S. Bose, *op. cit.*, p. 145, fn. 113.
91. *Kadambari*, para. 44.
92. N.S. Bose, *op. cit.*, p. 145, fn. 115.
93. *Ibid.*, p. 146, fn. 116.
94. *Ibid.*, fn. 125.
95. *Sukranitisara*, IV, 4, 125-29.
96. T.P. Bhattacharya, *The Canon of Indian Art*, p. 231.
97. *Ibid.*,
98. *Ibid.*, p. 232.
99. Kapila Vatsyayan (ed.), *Prakṛti*, p. 143.
100. *Ibid.*, p. 148.
101. *Ibid.*

7

Resume

The Chandellas of Jejakabhukti were the most important ruling dynasty of early medieval India. They were great rulers and builders of their times. They decorated their kingdom with the magnificent temples of Khajuraho. The temples of Khajuraho are world famous for their magnificence, proportion, perfection of design and sculptural profusion, which makes them masterpieces of architectural and sculptural art.

The Chandella artists did not rest with merely construction of temples. They added in them a new technique. Their temples are noble, imposing structures creating an impression of massive beauty. The gods, goddesses, *apsaras*, men and women standing or seeming to be in action, with their well-developed and voluptuous bodies, stand liberated from their stony frames, to emerge in a living world. The Chandella art of Khajuraho is a world of beauty, as would appear from the sculptural depiction of *apsaras* in their different moods. It appears very beautiful from the sculpture of the letter-writing woman. It surpassed many contemporary sculptural centres of art in portraying the different moods of men and women in stone and making even the pose of the figure a medium for the expression of mood.

The *apsaras* of Khajuraho are gay. The reminiscent mood is expressed in one sculpture. Another expresses the indolent mood; a third shows anxiety to get ready; a fourth, keenness to adorn herself, and a fifth, anxiety to do so. Still another figure describes tense attention in removing a thorn from the foot. The women with the mirror are lost in self-admiration. Their complacent smile and the intent eyes fixed on their reflection show them as the entinal women as they stand before a mirror. These beautiful sculptures which were carved by the Chandella artists on the walls of Khajuraho temples reflected the contemporary social environment, which inspired the artists to create various moods of youthful *apsaras*.

Before evaluating the reflection of environment on Chandella art and architecture, we have to consider the geographic position of Jejakabhukti region. The beautiful natural surroundings of this region greatly inspired the Chandella artists who were masters in the depiction of human and animal life in its multifarious forms. When we compare the contemporary art of the other dynasties with the art that developed in Central India, we notice the significant part played by nature in the Chandella art and architecture. The geographical configuration largely influenced the art and architecture of the Chandellas. The kingdom stood very close to the fertile region of north-western India, which lay to the north of the Yamuna and the Ganga, while the country itself, divided by numerous ranges of hills, the spurs of the Vindhya mountains, made it almost impregnable. The position of the Chandellas was further strengthened by the possession of the important and almost inaccessible forts of Ajaigarh, Mahoba and Kalanjara.[1] The region is also known for its numerous rivers and lakes, formed by erecting embarkment across the rivers. The region is very rich in natural resources, and being traversed by many branches of the Vindhyas and still many more rivers, rivulets and forests, it is famous for its natural surrounding and beauty which attracted the notice of Chandella sculptors who decorated it in their art and architectural creation.

Thus, geographical environment influenced the physical and mental creativity of a concerned region. The mountains of the region are reflected in the temples of Khajuraho. The architects of Khajuraho constructed their free-standing temples just like the replicas of mountains. This is also reflected in the Chandella inscriptions of Khajuraho, which compare the height of Khajuraho temples constructed during the time of Chandella rulers with snowy peaks of Himalayas.[2] Similarly, one inscription from Ajaigarh compares the temples with mountain Kailasha.[3] Thus, we find the reflection of surrounding mountains in free-standing Khajuraho temples. The temples of Khajuraho look like mountains. This is a unique feature of Khajuraho temples.

The mountain rocks of the Jejakabhukti region provided the artist the material for the construction of temples, tanks, ponds and sculptures. The sculptors utilised the rocks of Kalanjara, Ajaigarh, Mohaba and Deogarh for carving their sculptures. The numerous sculptures carved by the sculptors at Ajaigarh and Kalanjara belong to rock art. At Kalanjara Chandella artists carved several rare and unique images on the rocks.[4] Thus, the Chandella artists utilized rocks for their beautiful artistic creations. In this way the artists saved valuable time and energy for carrying stone slabs from distant places. Thus, geographical environment is reflected in the rock-cut sculptural and architectural remains of Ajaigarh, Kalajara, Mahoba, Deogarh and other places.

The stone quarries of Panna provided fine sandstone for construction of temples and sculptures at Khajuraho. A panel kept in the Archaeological Museum depicts a large number of labourers carrying stones with the help of long wooden poles.[5] At Khajuraho, most of the temples and sculptures were constructed from the sandstone of Panna quarries. For such a large construction of temples, the Chandellas must have also utilized some other mode for transporting the stones. Thus, the Chandellas used the natural resources for construction of temples at Khajuraho. The diamond mines of Panna and adjoining regions equally added to the ruler's richness to construct high profile temples at Khajuraho[6] and other art centres. Thus, the natural resources of the region provided economic support for the construction of magnificent temples at Khajuraho. The geographical environment factor played an important role in the study of art and architecture of any region. The same is true for Chandella art and architecture.

In the Chandella art and architecture animals, birds and aquatic animals find a significant place. The animals were associated with men from earliest times. The animals were also associated with great qualities, rare even in men. They have been mentioned as full of wit, capable of appreciation and resentment, and sometimes sacrificing, heroic and noble. All these qualities in animals and birds have formed the themes of delightful depiction in art. Some animals are the embodiment of strength and majesty; lions, tigers and elephants represent this category. This includes the *Vyala*, a fabulous creature with a lion's body and the head of different creatures such as an elephant, a boar, a parrot and others. The *Vyala* is the typical art motif of medieval temple and is a very popular decorative motif at Khajuraho. Elephants are carved in a row on the basement of the Lakshman temple and as large figures in the ground, at the entrance of the Vishvanatha temple. This depiction of elephants in large number in Chandella temples reflects that during the time of Chandellas, elephants were found in large numbers in the forests of the region. The Chandella inscriptions also invariably refer to elephants. The Chandella army was strong, gallant and well-equipped[7] with elephants. One of the most significant animal representation is Nandi, Siva's bull carved from a single stone and installed in a Nandi *mandapa,* in front of the Vishvanatha temple constructed by the Chandella king Dhangadeva. Similarly, Varaha finds a prominent place in Chandella art. We find depiction of Varaha in various places in Chandella art. The most magnificent image of Varaha is installed in a separate temple facing the famous Lakshman temple. The Varaha image is carved on a single piece of solid sandstone. This Varaha image carries on its body more than six hundred seventy-five miniature figures in twelve carved rows. This huge Varaha image was installed by the Chandella king Yasovarman as a mark of victory. Thus, the Varaha image reflects the contemporary political environment prevailing during the time of the Chandellas.

The Chandella artists also depicted various hunting scenes in the temples of Khajuraho. They reflect the thick forests and wildlife existing at that time. We find depiction of various wild animals in these hunting scenes. During the Chandella period, hunting became a very important feature of the life of the ruling class as well as the aristocratic members of society.

The art of Chandellas, like that of other regions, reflects the environmental and socio-economic condition in their changing context and the people's behaviour. The art of Chandellas exhibits common upsurge of the people at large, including kings, aristocrats, priestly class, traders and the common peasantry, who strived hard and offered their best to lay down norms and develop various forms of sculpture, which were first experimented in Jejakabhukti region profusely.

The art of the Chandellas was based on native tradition which suited the socio-religious needs of an aristocratic feudal society. It reflects the contemporary trends and concepts prevailing during the time of Chandellas. The art acts here as a vehicle to carry all walks of life. The sculptures are depicted in such a simple manner that the onlookers can understand, enjoy and derive inspiration from them. The human figures, their dresses, ornaments and physical features, etc. are drawn from the living groups of people of the region. The background of the sculptural panels are filled with the various birds, animals and other decorative matters. The entire artistic panorama moves around the divine environment of Khajuraho. The popular beliefs and concepts of contemporary society is reflected beautifully in the sculptural art of Khajuraho. This unique identification of self with the divine life probably made the Chandella art alive and brought it nearer to the common men. It was this intrinsic and inherent quality of Chandella art which successfully attracted and inspired all the sections of society and common folk. The Chandella art, though aristocratic and sophisticated, also depicted the joys and sorrows of common people. It is not only royal personages but people at large, i.e. townsmen, ascetics, artisans, labourers, merchants, forest dwellers, and common folk who find their place in the sculptural art of the Chandellas. Similarly, the construction of Chandella temples generally depended on the wishes of royalty and the local needs of the people. But we cannot assign the construction of temples and monuments to only one class of people. Krishna Deva[7] assigned the temple construction of Khajuraho from Yasovarman to Vidyadhara. From inscriptional sources, we know that queens, high officials, rich merchants, religious teachers and common men also played an important role in the construction of temples and monuments.[8] The artisans and labourers also made a significant contribution to the construction of temples. The sculptors with their excellent skill and imagination created a world of unsurpassed sculptures. Similarly, the common labourers also made their contribution by putting their labour. The royalty also made a significant contribution by patronizing and inspiring the artisans. Thus, we can conclude that in art activities, all the sections of society made their contribution according to their position. To sum up, we may say that Chandella art is a composite effort of all the sections of society.[9]

The significance of Chandella art may be accounted for its reflection of contemporary environment, related to natural, political, socio-religious, economic, traditions and beliefs of the common people. The Chandella sculptor, who drew inscription from living models of the Chandella society, has made a very realistic depiction of contemporary social customs, manner, dress and ornaments. The Chandella art represents and reflects the contemporary life and culture in its full form.

The Chandella artisans were conscious of the rich and variegated forestry, wildlife, flora and fauna of their region. The innate love of nature exuberated everywhere through the artistically carved lotus flowers, garlands, creepers, plants, birds and animals, which dominate the moving panorama of Chandella art. The birds, animals and human beings are entwined to flow continuously in the same stream of life. It is a common vigour of life which flows through every thing, making them thrive and prosper. Not only the flowers and creepers are beaming with this eternal energy but the males and females, with their mannerable bends in body, are swaying a rhythm. The two (*dvibhanga*) or three bends (*tribhanga*) of the body of *apsara*s figures of Khajuraho like the meandering creepers suggest the nature's replication in the creativity of Chandella artisans. Women received an important place in Chandella sculptural art. She occupied a significant place in Chandella society as mother, wife and daughter. The Chandella queen played an important role in various aspects of life during the Chandella period. The inscriptions throw some light on the position of the queen during the reign of Chandellas. The Chandella inscriptions refer to Kanchuka, Puppa, Satyabhama and Kalyanadevi. They played an important role in different fields.[10] Similarly, Kalanjara inscription refers to the name of Mahanachni Padmavati along with Mahapratihara Sangram Singh. This inscriptional reference refers to her respectable position during the reign of Chandellas. The reference is significant from this point that during the Chandella period dancing was closely associated with temple worship and also indicates their hierarchical position. We find various depictions of musical and dance performance in the sculptural art of Khajuraho. This indicates the popularity of dance and music during the reign of the Chandellas, which reflects in their art.

The sculptors filled the Chandella art form with resilient vigour and breath of life. The artist depicted all forms of life as one and his art expressed the urge for integration. We can conclude that the Chandella artist created a universe through his creation. This can be expressed in the words of Banabhatta as '*Darsit Visvarupa*'.

NOTES AND REFERENCES

1. N.S. Bose, *History of Chandellas*, p. 172.
2. *Epigraphia Indica*, Vol. 1, pp. 122-135; 137-147; and 147-152.
3. *Ibid*., Vol. XXX, pp. 87-90.
4. S.K. Sullerey, *Ajaigarh Aur Kalanjara Ke Devapratimayain*, pp. 193-194.
5. H.D. Sankalia, 'Socio-Economic Background of Khajuraho', *Journal of Indian History*, p. 136.
6. *Ibid*., pp. 129-142.
7. Krishna Deva, *Khajuraho*, pp. 5-7.
8. Devangana Desai, *Khajuraho*, p. 7.
9. S.K. Sullerey, *Chandella Art*, p. 31.
10. S.K. Sullerey, 'Dimensions of Indian Womenhood', *Chandella Queens*, pp. 233-235.

Genealogy of the Chandella Dynasty

1. Nannuka (831-845)
2. Vakpati (845-865)

3. Jayasakti (865-885)
4. Vijayasakti
5. Rahila (885-905)
6. Harsha (905-925) = Kanchuka
7. Yashovarman (925-950) = Pushpa
8. Dhanga (950-999)

Krishnapa = Asarva

Devalabdhi

9. Ganda (999-1002)
10. Vidyadhar (1003-1035) = Satyabhama
11. Vijayapala (1035-1050) = Bhuvanadevi
12. Devavarman (1050-1060)
13. Kirtivarman (1060-1100)
14. Sallakshanavarman (1100-1110)
15. Jayavarman (1110-1120)
16. Prithvivarman (1120-1128)
17. Madanavarman (1128-1165) = Valhanadevi

= Lakhamadevi

= Chandaladevi

Yashovarman

Pratap

18. Paramardideva (1165-1203)
19. Trailokyavarman (1203-1245)
20. Viravarman (1245-1285)
21. Bhojavarman (1285-1288)
22. Hammiravarman (1288-1308)

Bibliography

SANKRIT, PRĀKRIT AND APABHRAṂŚA WORKS

Agni Purana, Anandashram Series, Poona, 1900.

Aparājitaprchita by Bhuvanadeva, ed. with introduction by P.A. Mankad, GOS No. CXV, Baroda, 1950.

Arthashastra, ed. R. Shamshastri, Mysore, 1929.

Ashtadhayayi, ed. Manish Chand Basu, Varanasi.

Beni Madhava, *Balabhadra-Vilas*, Lakhimpur, 1890.

Bhagavata Purana, Lakshmi Venkatesvara Steam Press, Kalyan, Bombay, 1929; Eng. tr. in 5 vols. by G.R. Tazare, Motilal Banarsidass, Delhi, 1973.

Bhavishya Purana, Shri Venkatesvara Press, Bombay, V.S. 1958.

Bilhan, *Vikranankadeva-carita*, ed. G. Buhler, Bombay, 1875.

Brihat Samhita of Varahamihira, ed. M. Kern, Bibliotheca Indica, Calcutta, 1865; Eng. tr. by M.R. Bhatta, Motilal Banarsidass, Delhi, 2 vols., 1981, 1982.

Chanda Baradayi, *Paramala Rāso* (Mahoba Khanda), ed. S.S. Das, Varanasi, 1919.

Prthvīrāja Rāso, ed. M.V. Pandia and S.S. Das, Varanasi, 1904.

Devi Bhagavata Purana, Shri Venkatesvara Press, Bombay.

Devi Bhagavata, ed. R. Pandaya, 1956.

Garuda Purana, Eng. tr. in 2 vols., Motilal Banarsidass, Delhi, 1978, 1979.

Harivamsa, ed. R. Kinjaveadekar, Poona, 1936.

Hemchandra, *Kumarpala-carita*, ed. S.P. Pandit, Bombay, 1900.

Isanasivagurudeva Paddhati, ed. Ganapati Sastri, Trivandrum, 1920.

Jayanaka, *Prthviraja-Vijay*, ed. (i) S.K. Belvalkar, Calcutta, 1914-22, (ii) C.H. Ojha, Ajmer, 1941.

Kalhana: Rajatarangini, ed. (i) Sir A. Stein, Bombay, 1892, (ii) Pandaya R. Shastri, Kashi, 1960.

Karpūramanjari of Rajasekhara (in Prakṛti), tr. by C.R. Lanman, Delhi, Reprint, 1963.

Krsna Miśra: Prabodha-Candrodaya, ed. (i) Vasudeva Sharma, Bombay, 1917, (ii) K. Sambasiva Sastri, Trivandrum, 1936; Tr. Eng. J. Taylor, London, 1962.

Kurma Purāna, Kashiraj Trust Edition, Varanasi, 1971, Eng. tr. in 2 parts, Motilal Banarsidass, Delhi, 1982.

Lay of Alha, ed. Waterfield, 1923.

Linga Purana, Eng. tr. in 2 parts, Motilal Banarsidass, Delhi, 1973; Shri Venkatesvara Press, Bombay.

Mahabharata, Critical edition, Poona, 1942.

Mahabharata, Geeta Press, Gorakhpur.

Malavikagnimitra – by Kalidas (Trans. Tawney, Ed. Sitaram Chaturvedi, Varanasi, 1950).
Markandeya Purana, Eng tr. F.E. Pargiter, Calcutta, 1888-1905.
Matsya Purana, ed. Pandits of Anandashram, Poona, 1907.
Meghaduta, ed. E. Hultzch, London, 1911.
Merutungacarya: Prabandha-Cintāmani, ed. Jinavijaya Bani, Santiniketan, 1933.
Padma Purana, Anandashram, Poona, 1894.
Rupakasatakam, by Vatsaraja, ed. C.D. Dalal, C.O.S., Baroda, 1918.
Samarangana-Sutradhara of King Bhoja, ed. T. Ganapati Shastri, revised & edited by V.S. Agrawala, COS No. 25, Baroda, 1966.
Siva Purana, Critically ed. by Pushpendra Kumar, Nag Publishers, Delhi, 1986. Eng tr. in 4 parts, Motilal Banarsidass, Delhi, reprint, 1978.
Skanda Purana, Shri Khemraj, Shri Krishnadas, Bombay, 1909. Shri Venkatesvara Press, Bombay, V.S. 1966.
Somesvara: Kirtikaumudi, ed. A.V. Kathavate, Bombay, 1933.
Suktamuktawali, ed. E.V. Krishnamachari, Baroda, 1938.
Varah Purana, Eng. tr. in 2 parts by S.V. Iyer, Motilal Banarsidass, Delhi, 1985.
Vavan Purana, Shri Venkatesvara Press, Bombay.
Vayu Purāna, Anandashram, Poona, 1905.
Vishnu Purana, Shri Venkatesvara Press, Bombay, 1922.
Visnudharmottra Purana, Shri Venkatesvara Press, Bombay.
Valmiki: Ramayana, Geeta Press, Gorakhpur.

ARABIC AND PERSIAN WORKS AND THEIR TRANSLATIONS

Al Badaoni, *Muntakhab-ul-Tawarikh*, Tr. G.S. Ranking, Calcutta, 1898.
Al Birani, *Tahqiq mali'l-Hind*, ed. E.C. Sachau, Tr. E.C. Sachau, *Alberuni's India*, Delhi, 1964.
Al Gardizi, *Kitab zain-ul-Akhbar*, ed. M. Nazin, Berlin, 1928.
Al Utbi, *Tarikh-i-Yamini*, Lahore, AH. 1300. Tr. J. Reyonlds, London, 1858. (ii) J. Briggs, *Tarikh-i-Jirishta*, London, 1927.
H.M. Elliot and J. Dowson, *The History of India as told by its own Historians*, Allahabad.
Hasan Nizami, *Taj-ul-Maasir*.
Ibn-Battuta, *The Rehla of Ibn Battuta* (India, Maldives Island and Ceylon), ed. & tr. Mandi Husain, GOS No. 122, Baroda, 1976.
Ibn-ul-Athir, *Al-Tarikh ul-Kamil*, Bulak, 1874.
Minhaj-ud-din, *Tabaqat-i-Nasiri*, Calcutta, 1864.
Muhammad, *Tarikh-i-Firishta*, Lucknow, 1874.
Nizam-ud-din, *Tabaqat-i-Akbari*, Tr. B. De, Calcutta, 1927.

MODERN WORKS

Agarwal, K.L., *Khajuraho* (Hindi).
Agarwal, U., *Khajuraho Sculptures and their Significance*, New Delhi, 1964.
Agarwal, V.S., *Bhartiya Kala* (Hindi), Varanasi, 1977.
Altekar, A.S., *The Rashtrakutas and their Times*, Poona, 1934.
Anand, Mulkraj, *Khajuraho*, Bombay, 1968.
Awasthi, Ramasaraya, *Khajuraho Ki Dev Pratimayain* (Hindi), Agra, 1967.
Banerji, J.N., *The Development of Hindu Iconography*, Calcutta, 1956.
Banerji, R.D., *The Haihayas of Tripuri and their Monuments*, MASI, 23, Culcutta, 1931.
Beal, S., *Buddhist Records of Western World*, London, 1884.
Bhattacharya, P.K., *Historical of Geography of Madhya Pradesh*, Delhi, 1977.
Bhattacharya, T.P., *Vastuvidya*, Calcutta, 1963.
Bose, N.S., *History of Chandellas*, Calcutta, 1956.
Chakravarti, K.K., *The Art of Khajuraho*, New Delhi, 1985. (ii) *Khajuraho in Perspective*, Bhopal, 1994.

Crooks, *Tribes and Castes of North-Western Provinces and Oudh.*
Dey, N.L., *Geographical Dictionary of Ancient and Medieval India*, London, 1927.
Desai, Devangana, *Erotic Sculpture of India*, first pub. 1975; 2nd edn. Munshiram Manoharlal, New Delhi, 1985.
——, *The Religious Imagery of Khajuraho*, Mumbai, 1996.
——, *Khajuraho*, New Delhi, 2000.
Dhaky, M.A., *The Vyala Figures on the Medieval Temples of India*, Varanasi, 1965.
Dhama, B.L., *A Guide to Khajuraho*, Pub. by Chhatarpur states, Bombay, 1927.
Dikshit, R.K., *The Candellas of Jejakabhukti*, New Delhi, 1977.
Deva, Krishna, *Temples of Khajuraho in Central India.*
——, *Khajuraho*, Brijbasi Printers, New Delhi, 1987.
——, *Temples of Khajuraho*, 2 Vols., ASI, New Delhi, 1990.
Elliot, *Memories of Races of North-Western Provinces of India.*
Gangoly, O.C., *The Art of the Chandellas*, Calcutta, 1957.
Habib, M., *Sultan Mahmud of Ghaznin*, Aligarh, 1927.
Jaganik, *Alha Khanda*, N.K. Press, Lucknow.
Kane, P.V., *History of Dharmastra*, 5 Vols., BORI, Poona, 1930-62.
Kramrisch, Stella, *The Hindu Temple*, 2 Vols., 1946; reprint 1976, New Delhi.
Lal, Kanwar, *Immortal Khajuraho*, Delhi, 1965.
Majumdar, R.C. (ed.), *The Age of Imperial Kanauj*, Vol. IV, 1955.
——, *The Struggle for Empire*, Bombay, 1957.
——, *Ancient India*, Delhi, 1968.
Mishra, K.C., *Chandela Aur Unaka Rajatva Kala* (Hindi), Varanasi, 1954.
Mishra, P.K., *Khajuraho*, New Delhi, 2001.
Mitra, S.K., *The Early Rulers of Khajuraho.*
Nath, R., *The Art of Khajuraho*, New Delhi, 1980.
Nigam, M.L., *The Cultural History of Bundelkhand*, Delhi, 1983.
Pandey, A.P., *Chandell Kalina Bundel Khasla Ka Ithihas*, Allahabad, 1968.
Pandey, L.P., *History of Ancient Indian Science*, Vol. I, Delhi, 1996.
Pathak, V.S., *Smarta Religious Traditions*, Meerut, 1987.
Prakas, Vidya, *Khajuraho*, Bombay, 1967.
Prakas, Bhartandu (ed.), *Problem and Potentials of Bundelkhand* with special reference to water resource base, Delhi, 1998.
Pogson, W.R., *History of the Bundelas*, Calcutta, 1878.
Rao, T.A. Gopinatha, *Elements of Hindu Iconography*, 1916, Delhi (Reprint), 1971.
Ray, H.C., *The Dynastic History of Northern India*, Calcutta, 1931.
Russell, R.V., *Tribes & Castes of Central Provinces of India*, London, 1916.
Shah, K.K., *Ancient Bundelkhand*, Delhi, 1988.
Sullerey, S.K., *Kalanjara evam Ajaigarh Ki Deva Pratimayain* (Hindi), Delhi, 1987.
——, *Chandella Art*, New Delhi, 2004.
Tiwari, G.L., *Bundel Khanda Ka Itihasa*, Kasi (Hindi), 1990.
Tiwari, Maruti Nandan, *Khajuraho Ka Jain Puratattva* (Hindi), Varanasi, 1987.
Vatsyayan, Kapila (Gen. Ed.), *Prkrati*, New Delhi, 1993.
Yadav, B.N.S., *Society and Culture in Northern India*, Allahabad, 1973.
Zannas, Eliky and J. Auboyer, *Khajuraho*, Hague, 1960.

ARCHAEOLOGICAL REPORTS AND WORKS ON EPIGRAPHY

Cunningham, A., *Archaeological Survey Reports*, Vols. II, VII, X & XXI.
Fleet, J.F., *Corpus Inscriptionum Indicarum*, Vol. III.
Fuhrer, *Monumental Antiquities and Inscriptions in N.W.P. and Oudh*, 1891.
Sastri, Hiranand, *Catalogue of Archaeological Exhibits in Lucknow Museum*, Allahabad, 1915.
Trivedi, H.V., *Corpus Inscriptionum Indicarum*, Vol. VII, New Delhi.

GAZETTEERS, ETC.

Imperial Gazetteer of India.
Gazetteer of the United Provinces.
Gazetteer of Banda, Hamirpur, Jhansi and Jalann Distric in U.P.
Atkison, *Gazetteer of Bombay Presidency, Gazetteer of Punna, Chatarpur, Sagar, Tikamgarh, Datia, Gwalior,* pub. by State Govt., M.P, Bhopal.

JOURNALS AND PERIODICALS

Ancient India.
Annual Report of A.S.I.
Bharti, B.H.U., Varanasi, Bihar Puravida, Patna.
Epigraphia Indica, Ootacamund.
Indian Archaeology – A Review, Delhi.
Indian Antiquary, Bombay.
Journal of Asiatic Society of Bengal, Calcutta.
Journal of Asiatic Society of India, Mumbai.
Journal of India History, Trivandrum.
Journal of Art History Congress, Guwahati.
Journal of the U.P. Historical Society, Lucknow.
Marg (Khajuraho Numbers-3), Vol. X.
Proceedings of the Indian History Congress, New Delhi.
Shadh-Patrika, Udayapur (Rajasthan).
Puratan Journal of M.P. Archaeology, Bhopal.

Index